"For the power and the truth of this practice,
may all sentient beings be free of suffering
and the causes of suffering.
May all sentient beings be close to happiness
and the causes of happiness."

Traditional formula used for at least the last ten centuries
by the practitioners of the *Dzogchen* Tibetan Buddhist school
to dedicate their efforts – big or small –
to the greater wellbeing of all living things.

OpenMind Publishing - December 2008

ISBN-13: 978-1499250589

ISBN-10: 1499250584

Contact the author through piero@drparisetti.com

Visit the author's website at http://drparisetti.com

21 Days into the Afterlife

A scientific and literary journey
that may change your life

Piero Calvi-Parisetti, MD

OpenMind

Contents

Day 1 - Introduction

I didn't say it was possible. I just said it happened.
Sir William Crookes

You want to talk about the *afterlife*? Have you gone completely mad?

Well – actually I don't think so. In fact, I regard myself as a pretty normal person.

Oh, yes?

Oh, yes. Perhaps, because of my background and of my job, I might even be considered a touch more balanced and inclined to rational thinking than your average person.

Explain.

All right – I am a medical doctor, with postgraduate education in public health and disaster management. I have spent some fifteen years working in the management of large-scale international humanitarian operations, serving in various capacities for the International Red Cross and for the United Nations. A few years ago I left my active, operational engagement in this sector to start a late academic career: I am currently Professor of Emergencies and Humanitarian Action at the Institute for International Political Studies of Bocconi University in Milan, Italy, and a visiting professor at the universities of York (UK), Pisa (Italy) and Geneva (Switzerland, where I live). I am also the author of several books, articles and technical publications in my area of expertise.

No weirdo, then... What about getting a life?

Well - I am glad to report that I already have one - in fact a very happy life, which includes a lovely family, plenty of friends and a lifelong, active interest in the performing arts.

Why are you interested, then, in things that normally attract the psychologically fragile, the easily deluded and the socially marginal?

Oops... You may have to think again here. The things you and I are going to discuss - at quite some length, if you'll bear with me - have attracted the interest of some of the finest minds on the planet. The list, once you consider it, is quite impressive. It includes Nobel Prize winners, scores of world-class scientists and more PhD's than you would bother to count. How about that for the easily deluded and the socially marginal?

Mmm... The question remains, though, of how come you have got into this - excuse me - nonsense.

See - you show yourself the kind of attitude that I've had for practically all my life. I've always been deeply convinced that people would believe literally anything. White supremacy, the unavoidable final victory of the Marxist-Leninist revolution, the fact that if you kill infidels you end up in heaven surrounded by beautiful virgins - I don't want to single out any particular idea or person here, I'm just giving examples of things that may have very little rapport with reality but in which, given the right circumstances, people strongly believe. And they behave accordingly. To a large extent I still maintain this view, but I must admit that I was forced to reconsider some of my ideas in light of what I have learned in recent years.

You have become a believer yourself, then?

No, not really. Look at what I just said: I was talking about people believing things that have very little rapport with reality. I found myself - to my complete astonishment - learning things that have a very strong rapport with reality, despite being utterly unbelievable. The quote at the beginning of the chapter conveys perfectly well my position: the things I've been learning about defy common sense as much as they are inconsistent with the current worldview proposed by science. Nevertheless these things happen, repeatedly and - in most cases - verifiably. Incidentally, the quote is from one Sir William Crookes, one of Britain's greatest physicists, President of the Royal Society and, yes, psychic investigator.

You keep talking about "things"... Isn't it about time you explained yourself a bit?

Sure. Before that, however, let me ask you a question or two.

All right - fire away.

What colour are flies?

Black.

Are you absolutely convinced of that?

Positive.

Have you ever seen a fly other than black?

No.

Therefore flies can only be black.

Yes, definitely.

Good. Now, tell me - how would you feel if one day you saw a white fly. A normal, completely ordinary fly - just, you know, white. You are there, you are damn sure you are not hallucinating, and there is the fly - white.

Well... Gosh... I don't know.

That's fine. I don't want you to tell me. Just stay for a moment with that image: you and the white fly. And imagine the thoughts and feelings that would cross your mind. Take a minute or two.

OK. Well, that would be weird, I suppose.

Yes, pretty weird. Now tell me: would that one white fly convince you that, despite all you have always believed, white flies do indeed exist? Before answering, just remember the many radical revolutions in science that were originated by one, marginal, seemingly insignificant and totally illogical observation.

Like what?

Like, for instance, Einstein's general relativity. Newton's laws of mechanics served us spectacularly well for centuries: they describe in minute details the behaviour of objects in our everyday world and are perfect for the human scale of observation. They work and they make eminent sense. Pity that they are wrong. It took Einstein to examine some totally irrelevant (for our everyday life) observations such as minute variations in the orbit of planet Mercury to understand that Newton's laws do not accurately describe reality. Today, reality is described with an astounding level of precision by general relativity's distortion of the four-dimensional time-space continuum, something that seems to make very, very little sense. Now - back to the white fly: would that one observation convince you that white flies exist?

Well, yes, I suppose so.

OK, good, remember that's the one observation. Now imagine you see another one, then another, then you start looking for them seriously and you find dozens, hundreds, and finally thousands. What do you think? Are you definitely ready to reconsider your ideas about flies?

I would have to.

Good - you've got my point. Please keep this in mind, as what our conversation is going to be about is exactly that: white flies, thousands of them. Now, back to the "things"...

The things you say you've been learning about.

Yes, what I would call now "the result of seeing one thousand white flies". Fasten your seat belt, 'cause I am likely to rock your world.

OK then, go ahead.

4

First: our mind is not entirely dependent on the physical brain. A part of the mind shows what physicists call *nonlocal* and *nontemporal* behaviour: it can be conscious of events happening at a different location and in the future. This part of the mind can also transmit thoughts at a distance and can influence inanimate matter.

Second: human personality survives physical death and is capable of interacting with the physical world it has left behind.

Fine - that's exactly how I thought. All that is complete, utter, colossal nonsense.

Quite so. Like white flies. Only that, as I will be explaining to you, it's true.

Day 2 - What and Why

This may seem odd, but that is not my fault.
Bertrand Russell

I really, really don't think you'll go very far in convincing me.

I don't intend to convince anybody. You and I will be talking about evidence – real-life white flies. At the end, you will be drawing your own conclusions. On the contrary, as we talk, I would like you to continue to play the part of the skeptic. Not the hardline skeptic, though - the one who would not accept even the strongest evidence, simply on the basis that it contradicts what science tells us today. God knows we have enough of those... They make noise, and attack serious research on pure ideological grounds, a little like the Church used to do with folks like Galileo. They don't do any favour, in my sense, to the advancement of science nor to their fellow human beings. Please be an open minded skeptic instead. Do question the evidence I will present, do apply your intelligence and critical sense. And, at the same time, resist the temptation of "going overboard".

What do you mean?

I mean don't start accepting just anything in a non-critical way. Ignoring what the real terms of the problem are - that is, what controlled scientific studies and the most credible anecdotal evidence tell us - leads scores of people to quite literally believe anything in the so-called field of "paranormal".

The fact that a number of quite unbelievable things do happen to ordinary people does not mean that just *anything* can happen. Moreover, the fact that some individuals have extraordinary gifts does not mean that those gifts are common – quite the contrary, I would say.

Let me give you a couple of examples. If you Google the term "electronic voice phenomena" you will end up with over one million results. Disgracefully, the vast majority of those results link back exactly to the psychologically weak and the easily deluded that we were discussing before – people going around in cemeteries with tape recorders and thinking they can hear voices from the dead in the hiss when they play back the tape. This has nothing, absolutely nothing to do with the genuine but relatively rare examples of "EVP" and with the stunning experiments conducted in controlled laboratory conditions that we'll discuss later. Similarly, if I were to ask you now to give me a definition of "medium", you would probably come up with a patchwork of images ranging from "psychic detectives" allegedly solving murder cases to tarot readers and fortune tellers, all the way down to the crooks advertising in newspapers for magic spells capable of "bringing back the loved one in just one sitting". This is quite sad, almost tragic I would say: so many people, for a variety of reasons, take advantage of other people's gullibility... Real mediums, as we will see in due course, are rare. They do just one thing – they act as a bridge to the world of the deceased – and they do it only for one reason: to help people cope with the loss of loved ones. With real mediums, money is never an issue: if a medium charges money for a sitting, you can be practically sure it's a fake.

These two categories are what I see as "enemies": the obtuse skeptics on the one hand, and the scores of charlatans (including crooks and deluded believers) on the other.

You want me to play the open minded skeptic, then.

Precisely. And, to begin with, let's look at the tiny episode that got me started on this trail. As you will see, in the greater scheme of things, it can be considered totally marginal - almost a "non entity" compared with the things we'll be talking about. Nevertheless, it was important for me as it was an unexpected white fly. Totally unexpected and, well, unsettlingly white.

Did it happen to you?

No, it happened to my wife. She's the person I know best and trust most in the world. There's no point in me singing her praises here - just understand that, for me, anything she says carries the same value as a personal, direct experience I might have had myself.

OK.

Good. Just a few years ago, she happened to tell me this little story of her teenage days in Glasgow. We had never talked about such things. We both have what I would define a cultural interest in spirituality and feel a sense of affinity with the Buddhist teachings, but spooky, otherworldly things were simply not part of our interests and certainly not on the menu of our conversations. And then, one day, she comes up with this memory of hers. Let me bring her into the discussion now, and tell you the story herself.

> "I must have been about sixteen or seventeen at the time, as I was studying for my final exams at secondary school. Every night, as I was trying to get to sleep, I was kept awake by a persistent, rhythmic knocking on the wall just next to the headboard of my bed. At the beginning, it didn't bother me too much, but as time went on it really began to disturb me. I remember asking my Dad at breakfast time one day if he could hear it and he said it was probably a bird stuck in the loft and he would check it out. I said I thought it was highly unlikely – unless that particular bird was wearing clogs! However, he did, dutifully check out the loft, there was no bird and the knocking continued.
>
> He then investigated the pipes to see whether it was a plumbing problem – nothing could be found and the knocking continued. As time went on, my nights became increasingly sleepless as I tossed and turned to the knocking sound, but there was nothing to do. I just had to put up with it.

9

Then, one morning, as I made my way out of the house to school with my hand on the front door handle, either my Mum or my Dad called out something to me. I swung round to see what was wanted, and as I did so the bottom right hand corner of my coat caught the lid of a Chinese pottery ornament my Dad had recently purchased at a local market. As the lid tipped over, so did the bowl and its contents."

To my astonishment and consternation, I saw what looked like cigarette ash spill out from the bowl. Although my Dad was a smoker I knew he certainly wouldn't have used this precious ornament as an ashtray. At that moment, both my Mum and Dad came into the hall to check out the noise and the three of us looked at each other in silence. I immediately made a connection with the contents of that porcelain bowl and the knocking on the wall and concluded that this must have been the spirit drawing attention to something that wasn't quite right. My parents did the necessary and the knocking on the wall ceased from that day onwards."

Yes, it's a cute and somewhat odd story, but I must say that that didn't blow me away…

It wasn't intended to. It was just to explain how I got into all this. I know my wife very well, and could tell that this had made a serious impression on her. She could still feel the amazement after all those years. So, after we talked this thing over for a while, I decided to look up on the Internet if anything serious had been written on a subject on which I then had pretty much the same opinion as you have today. I found a book by one very reputable British psychology professor – a book and an author we'll come back to pretty soon – and, now, that blew *me* away.

In what way?

Hold on. We've got the next three weeks to talk about this. Let me just tell you that those 572 pages pretty much changed my entire outlook on life. And they were followed by nearly another 20,000.

What do you mean? Have you really read 20,000 pages of this stuff?

Yes, very nearly. And I still do, and can't get enough of it. Books, mainly, but also plenty of original scientific papers and a variety of reports. This is what I will be talking to you about. I will have to condense a staggering quantity of information and try to present it in a way that will enable you to make your own judgment.

I don't know. You are obviously not a fool and you have taken this thing very seriously. You've asked me to sit down and listen to you, and I will. I don't entirely understand, however, why are you taking the trouble of spending time with me, to let me know...

This is a very, very important subject, but we will come back to it at the very end of our conversations, if you don't mind.

Day 3 - Psi

Unless there is a gigantic conspiracy involving some thirty University departments all over the world, and several hundred highly respected scientists in various fields, many of them originally hostile to the claims of psychical researchers, the only conclusion the unbiased researcher can come to must be that there does exist a small number of people who obtain knowledge existing either in other people's minds, or in the outer world, by means as yet unknown to science.
Prof. H. J. Eysenk, Chair of the Psychology Department, University of London

Well, I must admit this quote is quite impressive.

Impressive for sure it is, but it is also somewhat misleading.

How so?

Professor Eysenk speaks of a small number of individuals having extraordinary capacities: this is true for certain features of psi. For many others, however, it is abundantly evident that we *all* possess some degree of capacity. The baffling nonlocal and nontemporal behavior which I already alluded to does not appear to be a characteristic of the mind of a few gifted individuals. Rather, it seems to be a basic feature of human mind, shared by everybody on the planet.

"Psi", "nonlocal", "nontemporal": on top of feeling quite skeptical, I now feel also quite confused.

You are very right - some explanation is in order now. Let's start with the title of this chapter – "psi". If you have a look on Wikipedia, you will learn that:

"Psi is a term for parapsychological phenomena derived from the Greek, *psi*, twenty-third letter of the Greek alphabet; from the Greek *psyche*, "mind, soul". The term was coined by biologist Benjamin P. Wiesner, and first used by psychologist Robert Thouless in a 1942 article published in the *British Journal of Psychology*. A term used to demarcate processes or causation associated with cognitive or physiological activity that fall outside of conventional scientific boundaries."

So "psi" equals "psychic powers"?

Roughly yes, but we have to be more precise. Psi phenomena fall into two general categories: the first involves perceiving objects or phenomena beyond the range of the ordinary senses, the second is mentally causing action at a distance. Parapsychology, as it is researched in a number of University departments around the world, describes a number of faculties generally described with the term psi. First of all, we have Extra-Sensory Perceptions or ESP, which include any manifestations of psi that appear to be analogous to sensory functions. It covers the phenomena of:

Telepathy: (*literally remote feeling/perception*) information perceived by one person is gained by another person when the sensory channels we currently recognise are unavailable. This is what is tested with the *zener cards* you may have heard about – one subject looks at the symbols on the cards and another subject, located in another room (or in another State or country…) tries to guess what the first subject is looking at.

Clairvoyance: (*literally clear seeing*) where a person appears to gain information about their environment when the sensory channels are unavailable. This is also called "remote viewing" and has to do with people describing places or objects they cannot actually see (often thousands of kilometres away…).

Precognition: (*literally pre-knowing*) where nondeductible information about a future event is acquired. Nondeductible means that the subject being tested has no way of knowing or guessing that a certain event is going to take place and yet, as we will see shortly, information about future events is indeed gained.

Then we have Psycho Kinesis or PK (literally *mind movement*) which includes phenomena in which a person appears to directly affect their environment through mental intention or even by their mere presence. Think of ESP as analogous to sensory functioning and PK as the psi equivalent to motor functioning. Traditionally, PK has been split into two categories:

Micro PK: applied to cases where instrumentation and/or statistical analysis is needed to determine if there is an effect (for instance, influence of microelectronic devices).

Macro PK: applied to cases where naked-eye observation suggests there is an effect.

An older term, **Bio PK** has been used in cases where the target system to be influenced is a living system. However, this has been largely replaced by the DMILS (Direct Mental Influence of Living Systems) acronym. **DMILS** currently covers a range of phenomena in which an organism appears to trigger a physiological or behavioural response in a remote organism, without any apparent channel of communication or influence.

To end with definitions, telepathy and clairvoyance are the mind's features that we define "nonlocal" or "outside space": a part of the mind appears to be within the physical brain of the subject and another part is somewhere else at exactly the same time. Incidentally, nonlocality is a well-known feature of subatomic particles, described by quantum physics and demonstrated through astounding experiments. Precognition is the feature that we define "nontemporal" or "outside time": a part of the mind lives the present and remembers the past, and a part is somewhat conscious of the future.

This is psi, then – no weeping statues, no alien abductions, no Atlantis mystery.

OK – that's clear. But it is also clear to me that it's all nonsense. I've read that none of this stuff has ever been proven to actually exist.

You – and whoever wrote what you read – are completely wrong. In fact, this "stuff" has been proven to exist by thousands of carefully designed experiments, amounting to *several million* individual trials over a period of nearly one century. Such experiments have been carried out by the same institutions and using the same well established methods employed by any other branch of modern science. Hear me well here: the experimental evidence accumulated so far is so significant that the current view – *shared even by the most hardcore skeptics* – is that there is no need of any additional proof that psi exists. Rather, current experiments are "process-oriented" and aim at answering questions such as "What influences psi performance?" and "How does it work"?

It is essential for me to make this point convincingly, so I have to ask you to be patient and bear with me as I take a small detour before coming back to psi. Do you know what meta-analysis is?

No.

OK, let's try to explain without getting too technical. Meta-analysis is a rather complicated statistical technique for combining the findings from independent studies. It is most often used to assess the clinical effectiveness of healthcare interventions and it does this by combining data from two or more randomised control trials. Let's make one example: you have probably heard that Aspirin is used in patients who have a heart condition in order to prevent blood clotting and lower the risk of myocardial infarction.

Yes, I have.

How was the effectiveness of this preventive measure initially assessed? Through the usual scientific method employed in such cases: some 25 Universities carried out clinical trials. The problem is that, although practically all trials showed that there was indeed a positive effect, statistics came in the way: in only five trials out of 25 it was certain that the positive effect was *not* due to chance. In the other 20 trials, the routine statistical analysis showed that the positive effects *might* have been obtained by chance. A reviewer who was skeptical of Aspirin's ability to reduce heart attacks might then have looked at these trials and remain unconvinced.

And here is where meta-analysis comes into place: such a technique was employed to review the Aspirin trials collectively, and the results were published in 1988 in the *British Medical Journal*. The outcome of the analysis was widely described in the news media as a medical breakthrough: when the results of all the studies are *combined* through meta-analysis, chance is clearly ruled out. Meta-analysis declared that Aspirin *is* indeed effective in reducing heart attacks, and, as we all know, Aspirin has been used worldwide for the last 20 years with excellent results.

Why are you telling me all this?

Because this is exactly what happened with psi experiments. Considered individually, psi experiments have been successful, but issues remained with repeatability and – especially – with the lack of a theory predicting psi effects. This has fuelled the skeptics' doubts for over a century. When studies are combined through meta-analysis, however, *there is no doubt that the psi effects are real*. Please make sure you understand this: the same, exactly the same scientific method employed by medicine, biology, chemistry, physics and any other branch of science proves beyond doubt that psi exists.

Wow! If what you say is true, I must admit that this looks indeed striking.

It's of course not me saying that. I've found the Aspirin example - as well as the description of many of the experiments that we'll be talking about shortly - in a remarkable book by Dean Radin, an American PhD who worked at AT&T Bell Laboratories and later at GTE Laboratories on advanced telecommunications and who's held appointments at Princeton University, University of Edinburgh and University of Nevada. In my opinion, the book is a bit heavy for the casual reader and will probably appeal to those with a scientific background and a basic understanding of statistics, but remains a highly recommended reading for anyone interested in this matter. The book is called *The Conscious Universe: The Scientific Truth of Psychic Phenomena* and was published in 1997 by Harper Collins.

OK, that's noted. You were speaking about experiments...

Yes, lots of them. So many, in fact, that we'll have – as always in our conversations – to limit ourselves to just a few, and we'll not able to describe them in great detail. Remember, however, that all what we'll be talking about has been published in scientific journals, so you will always be able to access the original articles if you want to know more. Also, you may want to refer to the book by Radin I just introduced, or to the many other excellent publications on the subject, including *Parapsychology: The Controversial Science* by Dr. Richard Broughton (Ballantine Books, 1992). Back to the actual experiments, let's start with telepathy.

You mean "mind reading"?

Yes, in a way. We can summarise the experimental techniques as follows: one person looks at one image and another tries to guess what he or she is looking at. In the beginning, a very simple method was used: the *Zener cards*. This is a set of 25 cards with five different symbols on them, designed in the 1930's by Karl Zener, an associate of parapsychology pioneers Dr. J. B. Rhine and Dr. Louisa Rhine of Duke University in North Carolina, USA. In the experiment, one person (the "sender") would thoroughly shuffle the deck and then tried to mentally "transmit" one card at a time to another person (the "receiver"). If the process was ruled by chance alone, you would expect the receiver to make five correct guesses per deck of 25 cards. To the astonishment of the experimenters, the studies carried out by the Rhines showed that there was a small but statistically significant number of "excess right guesses".

What do you mean by "statistically significant"?

Using exact binomial probability calculations, it is possible to determine how "improbable" it would be to guess an excess number of cards correctly. In one set of experiments, for instance, 2400 total guesses were made and an excess of 489 hits (correct guesses) were noted. The *probability of obtaining this outcome by chance is equivalent to odds of 1,000,000 to 1* and thus show significant evidence that "something occurred."

How did the story evolve?

By 1940, 33 experiments had accumulated, involving almost a million trials, with protocols which rigorously excluded possible sensory clues (including placing the subjects in separate rooms or even in different buildings). Imagine that in a number of experiments, the receiver was even prompted to make guesses *before* the target cards had actually been selected by the sender! (This in fact tests precognition much more than telepathy). 27 of the 33 studies produced statistically significant results - an exceptional record, even today.

However, good science (and the skeptic's flames) required the results obtained by Rhine to be replicated independently: in the five years following Rhine's first publication of his results, 33 independent replication experiments were conducted at different laboratories. 20 of these were statistically significant.

Finally, meta-analysis was done specifically for precognition experiments conducted between the years 1935–1987 by Honorton and Ferrari and published in 1989 in the *Journal of Parapsychology*. This included 309 studies, conducted by 62 experimenters, and showed relatively small but extraordinarily significant positive results: the probability of obtaining them by chance was one hundred thousand billion billion to one. As you see, the scientific evidence for precognition, the most provocative of all psi phenomena, stands on firm statistical grounds.

I must admit that I am quite puzzled.

Good. You are slowly beginning to get my point. You have come across your first white fly, and, like anybody, you feel puzzled. Can the whole thing really be a conspiracy? Did Universities engage in widespread fraud? Can all these researchers be sloppy or incompetent? Do statistics lie? Answer these questions yourself, using your intelligence and common sense. If your answers are "no", then you are probably looking at your first white fly. Reflect on this for a moment. Consider how your logic and your common sense tell you that the fly is there, and is white, and how this one, small, single element of evidence forces you to reconsider *a lot* of things.

Back to telepathy, now, as we have to pick another incredibly interesting set of experiments, among the many that have been conducted during the last century. I suppose you have never heard of the term *Ganzfeld*.

No, you are correct, I haven't. Is it German?

Yes, it is indeed a German word, meaning *whole field*. It both refers to a methodology to test psi, and to a raging debate that opposed researchers and skeptics for over 20 years. Let's look at the methodology first: subjects in a ganzfeld experiment lie comfortably, listening to white noise or seashore sounds through headphones, and wear halved ping-pong balls over their eyes, seeing nothing but a uniform white or pink field (the ganzfeld). By reducing sensory input, this procedure is thought to induce a psi-conducive state of consciousness. In the earlier experiments, a sender in a distant room viewed a picture or video clip. After half an hour or so the subject was shown four such pictures or videos and was asked to choose which was the target. In order to address the critics' concerns, the methodology was vastly improved in following years, introducing computerized control over the entire process and increasing the number of targets to 80 static ones (still images) and 80 dynamic ones (short audio-video fragments). Furthermore, the receiver subject was placed in a steel-walled, sound-proofed and electromagnetically shielded room. If no psi effect is present, and if results are ruled by probability alone, you would expect a "hit rate" of 25%: the subject would make on average four correct guesses every 16 images.

Now, let's look at the fascinating story of the experiments and of the intellectual debate. After the first ganzfeld experiment was published in 1974, other researchers tried to replicate the findings, and there followed many years of argument and of improving techniques, culminating in the 1985 "Great Ganzfeld Debate" between Honorton (one of the originators of the method) and Hyman (a well-known critic). By this time several other researchers claimed positive results, often with quite large effect sizes. Both Hyman and Honorton carried out meta-analyses but came to opposite conclusions. Hyman argued that the results could all be due to methodological errors and multiple analyses, while Honorton claimed that the effect size did not depend on the number of flaws in the experiments and that the results a) were consistent, b) did not depend on any one experimenter, and c) revealed certain regular features of ESP. In a "joint communique" published in 1986 the two agreed to disagree:

"We agree that there is an overall significant effect in this data base that cannot reasonably be explained by selective reporting or multiple analysis. We continue to differ over the degree to which the effect constitutes evidence for psi, but we agree that the final verdict awaits the outcome of further experiments conducted by a broader range of investigators and according to more stringent standards."

Researchers worked hard to attain such stringent standards and the ganzfeld studies achieved full scientific respectability in 1994 when Bem and Honorton published a report in the prestigious journal *Psychological Bulletin*, bringing the research to the notice of a far wider audience. They republished Honorton's earlier meta-analysis and reported impressive new results with a fully automated ganzfeld procedure - the Princeton autoganzfeld. In reaction to Honorton's successful experiments, Hyman, the arch-skeptic, was forced to offer a concession:

> "Honorton's experiments have produced intriguing new results. If independent laboratories can produce similar results with the same relationships and the same attention to rigorous methodology, then parapsychology may indeed have captured its elusive quarry."

Were experiments indeed replicated?

You bet. First, the Department of Psychology of the University of Edinburgh published five different reports including 289 individual experiments using Honorton's "rigorous methodology" (to use Hyman's words). Then replications were carried out by the Department of Psychology of the University of Amsterdam, by Cornell University, by the Rhine Research center in Durham, North Carolina, and by the Universities of Goteborg, Sweden, and Utrecht, Netherlands. The results of the six replication studies were perfectly in line with those reported by Honorton in 1994 and, very interestingly, consistent with the results achieved in earlier experiments with less rigorous methodologies.

What are the conclusions, then?

Please consider these figures and draw the conclusions yourself. From 1974 to 1997, some 2,549 ganzfield sessions were reported in at least forty publications by researchers around the world. Meta-analysis carried out on of all such studies shows a "hit rate" of 33.2%, whilst, as we said in the beginning, you would expect 25% if the results were obtained by chance alone. This result is unlikely with odds against chance beyond a million billion to one.

I am *really* confused now. I feel that you are talking about something very big, but, not being very scientifically oriented, I am not sure I fully understand the meaning of these numbers.

Actually, we are talking about something rather small. Ganzfeld experiments show that people identify roughly four correct images every 12, whilst chance would dictate four hits in 16. The difference is not extraordinary in quantitative terms, *but is definitely there*. Psi does indeed exist – *information perceived by one person can indeed be gained by another person when all known sensory channels are unavailable*. Do you understand?

Yes, I think I do.

Well – there's another white fly. What do you do? Do you feel like rejecting the scientific evidence? Think twice, because if you accept it – no matter how unbelievable and inexplicable in current scientific terms – you will be forced to start changing radically your worldview. And believe me – we have just started to scratch the surface.

Day 4 - More PSI

Despite the ambiguities inherent in the type of exploration covered in these programs, the integrated results appear to provide unequivocal evidence of a human capacity to access events remote in space and time, however falteringly, by some cognitive process not yet understood. My years of involvement as a research manager in these programs have left me with the conviction that this fact must be taken into account in any attempt to develop an unbiased picture of the structure of reality.

H. E. Puthoff, Ph.D.
Institute for Advanced Studies, Austin

Please have a look at the picture above. Tell me what you see.

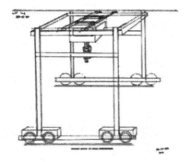

This looks like some sort of metal structure on wheels. I think I can make out rails beneath it and what appears like a winch hanging from the top part.

Thanks very much. Now look at this other one, and describe it for me.

It's the same kind of thing - a metal structure moving on rails. It's a gantry crane, like the things they use in ports to move around containers.

Excellent: it is indeed the same object, part of a super secret Soviet military installation at Semipalatinsk.

Very good. But why on earth are we looking at this now?

Well, the first image is a sketch made by a retired police commissioner named Pat Price, during a CIA-sponsored remote viewing experiment at Stanford Research Institute in Menlo Park, California, in July 1974. He was given only longitude and latitude coordinates of an unknown site on the other side of the world. The second image is a CIA artist's rendition of a satellite image of the same site.

You are just kidding me.

No I'm not. This was a remarkably accurate case, one of hundreds of tests conducted by the Stanford researchers. A full account of the experiment, coordinated by physicist Russell Targ, is available in the *Journal of Scientific Exploration.*

Were there more cases like that?
Look, if we start providing individual accounts of remote viewing experiments, we'll be here for weeks... This is my difficulty with our conversations: so much to say and relatively so little time. We'll have to pick here and there, among all the examples and the sources of information, and find something that makes my message come through.

24

As far as remote viewing is concerned, I would like to focus on another large and recent study and – oh, yes – another very public debate in which our friend Ray Hyman (you remember, the arch-skeptic?) had to concede. In 1995, the CIA commissioned a review of the government-sponsored remote viewing research that had been carried out during the previous two decades. The principal authors of the study were Dr. Jessica Utts, a statistics professor from the University of California, and Dr. Ray Hyman, then at the University of Oregon. The review included some 26,000 separate trials conducted at Stanford between 1973 and 1988 and a series of exceptionally rigorous experiments conducted between 1989 and 1993 by the Science Applications International Corporation (SAIC).

What were the results like?

Very, very interesting. Looking at the technical findings, for example, we learn that remote viewing is a rare talent: a small group of very gifted individuals far exceeded the performance of unselected volunteers. When mass screening of the population was carried out to find remote viewers, about 1% of the people were consistently successful. Astoundingly, neither the use of electromagnetic shielding nor the distance between the target and the viewer seemed to affect the quality of remote viewing. Also very interesting was the fact that neither training nor practice consistently improved performance. Remote viewing appears from this review to be a natural talent, distributed unevenly in the population like musical or athletic ability. Crucial to our discussion, however, are the conclusions. Here is what Jessica Utts wrote:

> "It is clear to this author that anomalous cognition is possible and has been demonstrated. This conclusion is not based on belief, but rather on commonly accepted scientific criteria. [...] I believe it would be wasteful of valuable resources to continue to look for proof. No one who has examined all of the data across laboratories, taken as a collective whole, has been able to suggest methodological or statistical problems to explain the ever-increasing and consistent results to date."

And what about the devil's advocate, Ray Hyman? After reviewing the same evidence, he concluded:

> "I accept Professor Utts' conclusion that the statistical results of the SAIC and other parapsychological experiments are far beyond what is expected by chance. The SAIC experiments are well designed and the investigators have taken pains to eliminate the known

weaknesses of previous parapsychological research. In addition, I cannot provide suitable candidates for what flaws, if any, might be present."

More white flies, then?

More than you can count, actually. Despite Dr. Utts' recommendation of not carrying out additional tests, the Princeton Engineering Anomalies Research Laboratory at Princeton University indeed carried out more remote viewing research, utilizing a different methodology. The results of the 334 trials showed positive results with odds of one hundred billion to one. *Remote viewing, like other PSI faculties, does exist.*

I feel like I'm slowly surrendering to the evidence. It's all so very confusing...

Confusing it is indeed – I fully understand you. Brace yourself, though, because we have just started to scratch the surface. We aren't done yet with PSI, and then we'll have to move into *way* more unbelievable fields of research...

Are we not done yet with PSI? I can hardly believe there's more...

There is a whole lot more, but we don't want to go too much in depth on the particular subject of PSI. Remember that I wanted to discuss parapsychology research with you first as I think of it as a good primer – a good method to get you thinking out of the box. Mind you – I didn't say *making you believe*, I said thinking out of the box. As I said from day one, I am just presenting evidence for you to consider. When we get to the really weird stuff, it will be *you* drawing the conclusions. For now, I find it interesting that you appear to be going through the same bewilderment I went through when I started studying these subjects.

Before we leave PSI, we still have to cover three areas of evidence, saving my favourite one for last. If I asked you to give me an example of "mind over matter" abilities, technically known as *psychokinesis,* or PK, what would you say?

Uh, I don't know. Probably I would think of the Israeli guy who said he could bend teaspoons with the force of his thoughts.

Oh, yes, Uri Geller. No, that's actually not what the evidence I have is all about. I don't know if he was ever tested under controlled conditions, and somehow I suspect he was not... Bending spoons is a big, very noticeable effect. You will have perhaps noticed that PSI manifests itself either with small effects across the entire population (like with the Zener cards experiments) or with relatively large effects produced by few gifted individuals (as in remote viewing). PK belongs to the first group: evidence shows that thoughts (anybody's thoughts) can actually influence inanimate matter, but the effect is minute, and becomes evident using sensitive, although unsophisticated, techniques. Let me explain how the thing works: do you know what a random number generator (RNG) is?

Yes – it is a device, or simply a computer program, that generates completely random numbers in sequence.

Very good. Now, given a large number of totally random generated numbers (say one million), what would be the share between odd and even numbers?

Very close to 50%.

Precisely. And this is exactly what happens if a hardware or software-based RNG runs on its own: as more and more numbers are generated, the share between odd and even numbers gets closer and closer to 50%.

Right, and?

And, when you ask volunteers to try to mentally influence the behaviour of a RNG (to "wish" that more odd or even numbers are produced), you get a small but phenomenally significant difference. 597 studies conducted by 68 different researchers consistently reported a share of about 51% in favour of the preferred option (odd or even). These overall experimental results correspond to odds against chance of one trillion to one.

Enormous numbers for a very small difference... Can you explain that?

Yes: you remember me having just said that the PK effects are minute. That one percent difference is certainly not a lot. That's not important, however – what is crucially important is that thoughts actually *can* and *do* influence physical processes, whilst all that contemporary science tells us about the nature of reality says they can't. How can we be so sure? Because of the extremely large odds against chance: it is fantastically improbable that that one percent difference just showed up by chance. So: the very same RNGs that constantly produce a 50% share when they are "left alone" constantly produce about 51% when influenced by thoughts, and this difference is certainly not produced by chance. What is the only conclusion?

That the difference is an effect of the volunteers' thoughts.

Bravo. You've got it. Like for other PSI faculties, it is evident that PK exists.

That's more and more amazing... Given that thoughts appear to be able to influence inanimate matter, what about influencing living things?

Yessir. That's exactly the point I was coming to. There is one study in particular that I found absolutely amazing. Do you know what a "double-blind" experiment is?

No, I am afraid I don't.

Poor you – I realize that more than a friendly discussion this is becoming a crash course in scientific method! Bear with me as I'll give a short explanation. Double-blind experiments are typically used to evaluate the effectiveness of new treatments in medicine. You take two groups of patients suffering from the same disease, to half of them you give a pill containing the substance you're testing and to the other half you give a placebo (a pill of the same colour and size containing no active substances). Nobody in the groups knows that they are been treated, and obviously nobody knows the difference between the active and the inactive pills – that's the first "blind". Then, at the end of the experiment, you have the clinical situation evaluated by an independent group of experts (not those who conducted the experiment), who obviously don't know who has been treated and who hasn't – that's the second "blind".

OK, I got the idea.

Good. In an often cited clinical study, in 1988 physician Randolph Byrd reported a double-blind study of intercessory prayer in coronary-care unit patients at San Francisco General Hospital. Byrd sent the names, diagnoses and conditions of 193 randomly selected patients to people of various religious denominations who were asked to pray for them. A similar group matched for age and symptoms was not prayed for.

Don't tell me that...

Yes, I do. The prayed-for patients turned out to be five times less likely to require antibiotics and three times less likely to develop pulmonary edema. None of the prayed-for group required endotracheal intubation, and fewer patients in the prayed-for group died.

But this is simply astonishing!

Yes, at face value it is.

Why only at face value?

Because, even if the study is strongly indicative that prayer indeed had an effect on the clinical history of these patients, from the methodological point of view it was not as rigorous as the thousands of experiments we've been talking about so far. I mean that it can be attacked by skeptics (and indeed it has been) who look for tiny loopholes in the methodology that could, with a stretch of the imagination, account for the results. For instance, the study was attacked on grounds of Dr. Byrd's own religious beliefs.

Here I ask you again to use your own judgment: how likely do you think it is that Dr. Byrd and his collaborators falsified the clinical records of hundreds of patients in an American hospital? And, if altering the records was not possible, could he have convinced the group of independent scientists who evaluated the data to change their interpretations? If data tampering and/or twisting arms occurred (think of the dozens of people involved…), how come that no information was ever leaked, by anybody? And how could a supposedly religiously-motivated study be accepted for publication by a reputable, peer-reviewed scientific journal? Please take a minute and ponder these questions yourself, and decide whether the Byrd study counts as yet another white fly.

It's now time that we turn to the experiment that has made the biggest impression on me. Can't see exactly why, but this has really blown me away. Perhaps is the simplicity of the technique, perhaps its ingenuity, perhaps the merciless essentiality of the results. Bang – in your face! No two ways of interpreting the data, no uncertainties. Now, let me ask you, if you happen to know, how the lie detectors used by the police work.

Yes, in fact I do know how it works. The principle is that when we lie we get somewhat more emotional, even if we think we are in control. That emotion shows through subtle physiological signs, including a small increase in skin transpiration. When the skin gets more moist because of transpiration, it conducts electricity better. This is the simplest version of a lie detector: sensors recording electro-dermal conductivity.

Very good! So, let's make sure we are on the same line: we get emotional (because we lie or for other reasons), we sweat a little more and the lie detector measures small variations in the skin conductivity.

That's exactly it.

Excellent. So we would expect that we would get emotional *after* something has made us emotional.

Yes.

Then follow me as I describe this experiment, because you're in for a big surprise. Imagine a person – the subject – looking at a computer screen. The screen shows nothing for five seconds, then one image for three seconds, then nothing for ten seconds, and then the cycle starts again with a different image. The images are selected at random by the computer from a pool of 900. 583 of them have no emotional value (landscapes, portraits, objects, etcetera) and the remaining 317 have an intense emotional connotation: explicit sex or violence. What would you expect after the subject has been shown neutral images?

Nothing much. The skin conductivity of the subject should remain largely unchanged.

And this is precisely what happens. Look at the graph below and concentrate on the line with the white markers. They trace the subjects' reactions during the cycles with emotionally neutral images. What do you notice?

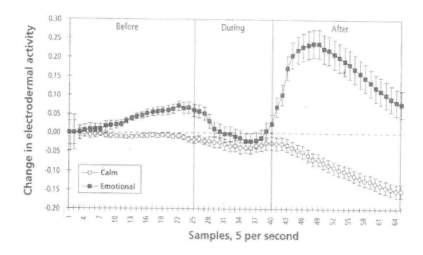

Samples, 5 per second

That the subjects are not particularly emotional before and during the period in which the images are shown, and then their emotional level goes down during the two five seconds periods of blank at the end of the cycle.

Very good. Apparently, skin conductivity goes down because subjects get bored. Now, look at the black dots, which trace the response to the cycles showing emotionally charged images. What happens after the images have been shown?

There is a big peak in skin conductivity. The subject get emotionally aroused and sweats.

Good – as you would expect. Now tell me: what happens *before* the images are shown?

There is a... BUT THIS IS IMPOSSIBLE!

I'm sorry. It may well be impossible but it's there to see. Somehow, the subjects' minds know that an emotionally charged image is going to be shown *before* it actually appears on the screen, and the body reacts in anticipation. This is pure nontemporal behaviour. This is precognition shown in laboratory conditions, at the University of Nevada, and replicated with exactly the same results by the University of Amsterdam.

Day 5 - Near-Death Experiences

I was still in the room, but instead of being sick in my bed I left my body and floated up to the ceiling. I saw my body like a dead pig dressed in my clothes. My children wept over me, and this caused me intense pain. I tried to talk to my family, but no one could hear me.

The subject of near-death experiences is not new, even to me. I've often read of people reporting experiences like the one quoted above. There are hundreds of books, news reports, documentaries, even a couple of Hollywood movies talking about that. It's no surprise that so many people report such experiences today - they are influenced by this overflow of information.

Umm... Please re-read carefully the quote. What do you notice?

Nothing special. It seems to me the typical near-death experience you would read about in a tabloid.

You mean the kind of thing lots of people think they have experienced because they're influenced?

Yes, exactly.

Well, the quote is from Lingza Choki, a Tibetan aristocrat who lived (and nearly died...) in the 16th century. That's a few years before tabloids.

Oh.

Oh, yes. Let's start by addressing this first, common misconception. Near-death experiences, which from now on we'll refer to as NDEs, are not a phenomenon of the last 40 years. They have been consistently reported by all civilizations throughout history. A very similar account, for instance, can be found in the Hammurabi Code from ancient Mesopotamia, dating back to ca. 1760 BC. This in itself is an enormously fascinating subject. If you are interested, a scholarly but very readable review is available from Oxford University Press (Zaleski, Carol. *Otherworldly journeys: Accounts of near-death experiences in medieval and modern times*. 1987).

You have surprised me again there. Can we start the NDE thing from the beginning, then?

All right. As usual, it is difficult for me to select points which are salient for our discussion amidst the ocean of available information. As I have done with previous subjects, I will select one particular source to get us started.

On December 15, 2001, the highly respected international medical journal, *The Lancet*, published a 13-year study of NDEs observed in 10 different Dutch hospitals. This is one of the very few NDE studies to be conducted prospectively, meaning that a large group of people experiencing cessation of their heart and/or breathing function were resuscitated during a fixed period of time, and were interviewed. Through those interviews the doctors discovered who had experienced NDEs and who hadn't. The advantage of this type of study is that it gives scientists a matched comparison group of non-NDE patients against which to compare the NDErs, and that in turn gives scientists much more reliable data about the possible causes and consequences of the near-death experience.

Of the 344 patients tracked by the Dutch team, 18% had some memory from their period of unconsciousness, and nearly 12% (1 out of every 8) had what the physicians called a "core" or "deep" NDE. The researchers defined that as a memory by the patient from their period of unconsciousness which scored six or more points on the scale published by Dr. Ken Ring in his 1980 study, *Life at Death: A Scientific Investigation of the Near-Death Experience,*. This scale includes:

- A sensation of floating out of one's body. Often followed by an out-of-body experience where all that goes on around the "vacated" body is both seen and heard accurately.

- Passing through a dark tunnel. Or black hole or encountering some kind of darkness. This is often accompanied by a feeling or sensation of movement or acceleration. "Wind" may be heard or felt.

- Ascending toward a light at the end of the darkness. A light of incredible brilliance, with the possibility of seeing people, animals, plants, lush outdoors, and even cities within the light.

- Greeted by friendly voices, people or beings who may be strangers, loved ones, or religious figures. Conversation can ensue, information or a message may be given.

- Seeing a panoramic review of the life just lived, from birth to death or in reverse order, sometimes becoming a reliving of the life rather than a dispassionate viewing. The person's life can be reviewed in its entirety or in segments. This is usually accompanied by a feeling or need to assess loss or gains during the life to determine what was learned or not learned. Other beings can take part in this judgment like process or offer advice.

- A reluctance to return to the earth plane, but invariably realizing either their job on earth is not finished or a mission must yet be accomplished before they can return to stay.

- Warped sense of time and space. Discovering time and space do not exist, losing the need to recognize measurements of life either as valid or necessary.

- Disappointment at being revived. Often feeling a need to shrink or somehow squeeze to fit back in to the physical body. There can be unpleasantness, even anger or tears at the realization they are now back in their bodies and no longer on "The Other Side."

Yes, this very much corresponds to what I have heard on NDEs. The first explanation that comes to mind is that these are hallucinations produced by a dying brain. It seems quite possible to me that a mind deprived of oxygen would start producing fantastic images...

Have you ever tried LSD yourself?

Oh, God, no!

Have you ever worked with schizophrenic patients?

No - of course not.

Well, if you did – try LSD or know about the delirium of schizophrenic patients – you would know that hallucinations indeed belong to the same category of experiences as those reported by NDErs.

You see?

No, wait a moment. I am not saying they are the same thing, I'm just saying they belong to the same category of experiences. There are three main objections that invalidate the hallucinatory explanation of NDEs. First: anybody familiar with drugs- or psychosis-induced hallucinations knows that they come in an infinite variety of forms. No two acid trips are ever equal, no two schizophrenic patients report the same hallucinations and very often the same patient goes through extremely different experiences. NDEs have an astounding degree of consistency: independently of age, race, education, religious beliefs, NDErs have reported the very same experience for the last 5,000 years. Second: if NDEs were indeed hallucinations produced by anoxia, why do only 18% of the patients experiencing anoxia report an NDE? Third and possibly most important: if you look at the electroencephalogram of a person experiencing hallucinations you see a very, often extremely active brain. The EEG of NDErs is flat – that's why they are considered clinically dead. How do you explain the richness of the experience with a brain showing no electrical activity? Even more astonishingly, how is it possible that an apparently non-functioning brain can activate the mechanism that supports long-term memorization (NDErs recall their experience with the same degree of detail when interviewed again several years later)?

I don't know... I have no explanations. Could it not be an effect of the drugs administered to the critically ill patient?

Then, how would you explain that patients who were given completely different drugs – or no drugs at all – report exactly the same experience? Let me quote Dr. Pim Van Lommell, the author of the Dutch study I mentioned before, to address some of the most common criticisms of NDEs.

"Our results show that medical factors cannot account for the occurrence of NDEs. All patients had a cardiac arrest, and were clinically dead with unconsciousness resulting from insufficient blood supply to the brain. In those circumstances, the EEG (a measure of brain electrical activity) becomes flat, and if Cardio-Pulmonary Resuscitation is not started within 5-10 minutes, irreparable damage is done to the brain and the patient will die. According to the theory that NDEs are caused by anoxia, all patients in our study should have had an NDE, but only 18% reported having an NDE... There is also a theory that NDE is caused psychologically, by the fear of death. But only a very small percentage of our patients said they had been afraid seconds before their cardiac arrest - it happened too suddenly for them to realize what was occurring. More patients than the frightened ones reported NDEs. Finally, differences in drug treatments during resuscitation did not correlate with the likelihood of patients experiencing NDEs, nor with the depth of their NDEs."

And.

And?

And, there is another extremely important fact that proves that NDEs are highly structured and highly consistent psychological experiences, miles away from drug induced hallucinations and from the fleeting "mystical" experiences that can be triggered by electrically stimulating certain parts of the brain.

What would that be?

A massive amount of research proves that in the realm of beliefs, values, behaviour and overall outlook on life, NDErs, however different they may have been before their experience, show astonishing similarities. Already in 1984, Dr. Kenneth Ring Ph.D. – then professor of psychology at the University of Connecticut and one of the leading experts on NDE research – summarized years of research by stating: "From a psychological standpoint, it was almost as if they had all undergone much the same initiatory ordeal – triggered by the trauma of nearly dying which then, unexpectedly, gave rise to the same life-transforming insights – and then emerged from it to speak in a single voice and act from the secret knowledge of a shared vision".

Since 1984, at least eight additional major investigations of NDE aftereffects in the US, England, Australia and Italy have provided further evidence of the stability of this pattern. If we were to summarise the psychological changes NDErs undergo we would come up with this list:

- Increased appreciation for life
- Increased self-acceptance
- Increased compassionate concern for others (in fact, not only for humans but for all other forms of life)
- Decreased interest for material goods
- Decreased competitiveness
- Increased spirituality (very interestingly, NDErs who were religious before showed a decrease in their interest for the formal aspects of religion and increased interest for a more universal and comprehensive spirituality)
- Increased interest in knowledge for its own sake
- Sense of purpose in life
- Virtual disappearance of the fear of death
- Belief in life after death
- Belief in God or in a superior being, sometimes referred to as "the Light"

Please appreciate that these beliefs and attitudes were all measured with time-proven psychometric methodologies and personality inventories.

Can I please have an NDE?

HA! You've got it! You've got it! I'm very excited! We're not even halfway through all the things I intended to tell you and you've already touched the very core, the absolute essence of our entire conversation!

Do calm down, please.

Yes, you are right, I'm sorry – I got carried away. But please understand how important this is for me. If you remember, on day 2, when you asked me why I bothered embarking on this exercise – the dialogue, the publication, and all the rest – I said that I wanted to wait until we covered all the subjects, and then I would explain. Now, instinctively, you've already jumped to the core meaning of all this.

The core?

Yes! I don't want to go in depth now - I still want to save my bottom line for the end. But just reflect briefly on one thing. You've heard about the life transformation that NDErs go through with a remarkable level of consistency after their experience, and what did you automatically think?

That it would be nice to have one. All the psychological changes you mentioned seem very desirable.

Yes, very, very good! They are indeed very desirable. Only, research shows that *you don't need to go near death and then come back to achieve such transformation.* There is solid evidence that just learning about NDEs can bring about these changes. The more people get to know about this particular subject and study it, the more these psychological changes become apparent, *without the need of having an actual NDE.*

This is interesting. I know that this happens in other fields as well. I know, for instance, that in the case of cognitive-behaviour psychotherapy, what they call *bibliotherapy* – I mean the study of reference books and self-help manuals – is as effective as formal psychotherapy sessions in the treatment of mild and moderate depression.

Well – that's an expert's comment. This is indeed the case. Now, ask yourself - if just learning about the NDEs can bring about positive psychological changes, what about learning about the whole shebang – from PSI to NDE, from mediums to instrumental transcommunication, from energy-based phenomena to reincarnation studies? Wouldn't the changes be more profound, more long-lasting, more life-transforming?

Now, back to our subject of the day – NDEs. We have to reflect on one important thing – the reality of such experiences.

What do you mean?

I mean that, based on the evidence we have discussed so far, we have in a way to take something merely on faith – faith on the accuracy of somebody else's judgment.

Sorry, but I still don't understand...

Yes, what I want to say is that all NDErs provide an essentially unanimous judgment of their experience. For them it's no dream or hallucination, many say that their NDE was "more real than life itself". However, no matter how impressive the unity of this judgment across time, personality, language, culture, religion, the experience as we described it so far remains unverifiable and rests on subjective self-reports. How do you think such experiences could be verified?

Umm... let me think. A lot of the NDE content seems to be visual. NDErs typically describe, at the early stages of the experience, their body, their immediate surroundings, the people around them... If what they report corresponds to reality, that would be a form of verification.

That's true, but I think that's a weak form of verification. Such images could be based on the last memories they formed before losing consciousness, and on imagining, like in a realistic dream, what is happening. You are on the right track, but you have to think harder and give me a better verification method.

Let me think again... What if they report having seen something that they could not have seen from their bed?

Exactly! That's a good form of verification.

Has this happened?

Of course it has. Let me tell you an anecdote, and then we'll look at some research findings. A well-known case is reported by Kimberly Clark, a critical care worker at Harborview Hospital in Seattle, who contributed a chapter to a scholarly book on the subject published in 1984 (B. Greyson, C.P. Flynn (Eds.), *The near-death experience: Problems, prospects, perspectives* , Springfield, Il, Charles C. Thomas). The case involves a woman named Maria, a migrant worker who suffered a heart attack whilst visiting relatives in Seattle and went through a cardiac arrest whilst in the coronary care unit. After having been resuscitated, Maria reported to Clark having had an NDE.

Clark, who had heard of NDEs but was skeptical of them, listened with what she described as "feigned but seemingly emphatic respect" to the patient's account of the experience. Clark reports that, inwardly, she was finding plausible explanations to dismiss the various elements of a fairly typical NDE account, until Maria mentioned something bizarre. At a certain point, Maria told Clark that she did not merely remain looking down from the ceiling, but she found herself *outside* the hospital. Specifically, she said, having been distracted by an object on the ledge of the third floor of the north wing of the building, she "thought herself up there". And when she "arrived" she found herself, as Clark put it, "eyeball to shoelace" with – of all things – a tennis shoe on the ledge of the third floor on the north wing of the building! Maria then proceeded to describe the shoe in minute detail, mentioning, among other things, that the little toe had a worn place in the shoe, and that one of its laces was tucked underneath the heel. Maria herself got emotional, and insisted that Clark should try to locate the shoe as she desperately needed to know whether she had "really" seen it.

The north face of Harborview Hospital is slender, with only five windows showing from the third floor. When Clark arrived there, she didn't find any shoe – until she came to the middlemost window on the floor, *and there, on the ledge, precisely as Maria had described it, was the tennis shoe.*
The question here is: What is the probability that a migrant worker visiting a large city for the first time, who suffers a heart attack and is rushed to a hospital at night would, while having a cardiac arrest, simply "hallucinate" seeing a tennis shoe – with very specific and unusual features – on the ledge of a floor *higher* than her physical location at the hospital?

Clark herself wrote: "The only way she could have had such a perspective was if she had been floating right outside and at very close range to the tennis shoe. I retrieved the shoe and brought it to Maria; it was very concrete evidence for me."

Wow!

Yes, wow! And, as usual, there are plenty of stories like this one. We have to move into research now, as – yet again – this provides evidence for more white flies. In his book *Recollections of death: A medical investigation* (New York: Harper and Row, 1982) cardiologist Michael Sabom reports on his careful and systematic work. The first part of the research consisted of collecting data: Sabom used detailed protocols to interview patients who reported visual experiences while undergoing cardiac surgery or in connection with cardiac arrests. He then went on to consult with members of the medical teams and other witnesses, and also examined the clinical records of these patients, in order to determine to what extent these perceptions could be verified. In most instances, Sabom was able to provide compelling evidence that these patients were reporting precise details concerning their operation, the equipment used, or characteristics of the medical personnel involved, which they could not have known about by normal means.

The second part of Dr. Sabom's investigation consisted of a control procedure, devised to further test the reality of what the patients reported. He identified 25 chronic coronary care patients who had never been resuscitated, and asked them to *imagine* what the procedure would be like as if they were a spectator of their own resuscitation, much like the NDEers experience. The results from this control group were intriguing, to say the least. 22 of his 25 control respondents gave descriptions of their hypothetical resuscitation that were riddled with errors; their accounts were often vague, diffuse, and general. According to Sabom, the reports from patients who had actually been resuscitated were *never* marred by such errors and were considerably more detailed as well.

Seeing and remembering whilst unconscious... This is so damn incredible!

Hang on, my friend. We haven't yet talked about the *really incredible* piece of evidence concerning NDEs. Can you imagine what that could be?

No, not really.

Tell me: what would you call somebody who can't see?

A blind person. Now, you are not telling me...

Again, I am afraid it's a yes. Either you bother to read a technical paper (Ring, K., Cooper, S., "Near-death and out-of-body experiences in the blind: A study of apparent eyeless vision", *Journal of Near-Death Studies*, 16, 1997) or you bear with me telling you.

I'll settle for you, but I feel dizzy already.

All right, then, fasten your seat belt! What Kenneth Ring and his co-researcher Sharon Cooper did was to ask for help from eleven American Associations for the Blind. They even published a newspaper advertisement in order to find subjects to be included in the research. After extensive screening, they ended up with 21 subjects who met the study criteria - blind individuals who had had conscious experiences associated with unquestionably life-threatening conditions. Nine of the 21 subjects had lost their sight after age five and were classified by the researchers as "adventitiously blind". Two were severely visually impaired and the remaining ten had never experienced vision, however limited.

The in-depth interviews the researchers carried out with the subjects established that five out of the ten people who were blind from birth could actually experience vision during their NDE. The other five either had no sight or were unsure whether they had sight or not. Of the 11 adventitiously blind or severely visually impaired, all but one reported what seemed to be normal vision during the NDE.

Well, obviously they were dreaming!

No they were not. Not only the subjects reported that the experiences were completely different from their dreams, but extensive research with the congenitally blind assures us that they have no vision whilst dreaming, and indeed that there is very little vision in the dreams of those who have lost sight early in life. The congenitally blind normally dream of sounds and tactile sensations; the blind NDErs were adamant that they were seeing during their experience, including having the overwhelming shock of seeing their own body for the first time.

But, how could a congenitally blind person know what "seeing" is all about?

Very good point! In some cases, members of the study group were pressed on this subject by the researchers. They reported that their "seeing" was a form of awareness, a sort of expanded tactile experience, although no touching was actually involved. They used the word "see" because that is in the linguistic convention. Ring and Cooper, however, point out that the insistence on "brightness" and the frequent reference to colours seem much more related to vision than to touch. Furthermore, you must know that some non blind people report having what is called "mindsight" during their NDEs. They seem to be able to see through 180 degrees at one and the same time, and to see through doors, walls and other apparently solid objects. The fact that some of the blind people in the study independently reported the same experience is considered highly evidential.

Seeing through doors and walls? I'm afraid you're losing me here...

No, no stay with me just now. We'll talk about research on mindsight another time. For now, let's stay focused on blind people actually seeing during an NDE. Another explanation that the researchers considered was that the subjects constructed an imaginary experience from auditory information heard before or immediately after the NDE.

Yes, that seems reasonable...

...but doesn't explain those accounts in which members of the group reported "seeing" during their NDE unusual objects or events that would not feature in auditory information. Think, for instance, of the subject named Nancy, tragically and permanently blinded by a mistake during a surgical operation. While Nancy was in the recovery ward after the operation that cost her sight, the medical staff understood that there were complications. She was taken out of recovery room and wheeled to have an angiogram. At this point, she regained consciousness, realized she had lost sight, and immediately found herself out of her body. From that position, she was able to "see" again much that happened to her on the way to the angiogram, including "seeing" her then lover Leon, and Dick the father of her child standing further away down the corridor. She then went into what she describes as "the light", where she was persuaded to return to her body. Medical records essentially confirm the external aspects of these experiences, but the best confirmation came from Leon. When he was independently interviewed by the researchers, he provided an account of his actions that corresponded in every important detail with what Nancy reported.

Wow...

I know. Amazing, isn't it? I have saved the best piece for last, however. It is not necessarily the strongest or the most extraordinary, but it's so *beautiful* that it made a big impression me. Two of the case studies of those born blind, those of Vicki Umipeg and Brad Barrows respectively, contain accounts of particularly clear vision of both earthly and "paradise" conditions during the NDE. Vicki found the experience disorientating, whilst Brad was less worried, and his descriptions are striking and precise. He comments for example on the "brilliance" of the colours, more "brilliant" than any of the descriptions of colour given to him by sighted people.

At some stage, Brad provides a description of the "very soft snow" he "saw" when his consciousness was apparently out of the body and above the street during the NDE. It is so simple, in a way poetic, and so overwhelmingly beyond anything that could be fabricated that it makes my eyes well with tears every time I read it. Brad, born blind, says:

> "It had not been covered with sleet or freezing rain. It was the type of snow that could blow around anywhere. The streets had been ploughed and you could see the banks [of snow] on both sides of the streets. I knew they were there. I could see them."

Day 6 - Deathbed visions

I want to start by telling you the story of Professor Barrett, because it somehow resembles mine.

How so? And who's Professor Barrett anyway?

You'll remember that what got me started in my research about the afterlife was an almost insignificant episode recounted by my wife.

Yes, the rapping in Glasgow – I remember.

Good. Sir William Barrett was a professor of physics at the Royal College of Science, in Dublin in the 1920s. He too had a wife who one day told him a funny story, a story that interested him so much that he was to go on and become one of the most prominent psychic researchers.
Sir William's wife was a gynaecologist at Dublin's main hospital and, on the night of January 12, 1924, she arrived home from the hospital eager to tell her husband about a case she had had that day. She had been called into the operating room to deliver the child of a woman named Doris (her last name was withheld from the written report). Although the child was born healthy, Doris was dying from a haemorrhage. As the doctors waited helplessly next to the dying woman, she began to see things. As Lady Barrett tells it:

Suddenly she looked eagerly towards part of the room, a radiant smile illuminating her whole countenance. "Oh, lovely, lovely," she said.

I asked, "What is lovely?"

"What I see," she replied in low, intense tones.

"What do you see?"

"Lovely brightness, wonderful beings."

It is difficult to describe the sense of reality conveyed by her intense absorption in the vision. Then - seeming to focus her attention more intently on one place for a moment - she exclaimed, almost with a kind of joyous cry:

"Why, it's Father! Oh, he's so glad I'm coming; he is so glad. It would be perfect if only W. (her husband) would come too."

Her baby was brought for her to see. She looked at it with interest, and then said:

"Do you think I ought to stay for baby's sake?"

Then, turning toward the vision again, she said:

"I can't - I can't stay; if you could see what I do, you would know I can't stay."

Now – Sir William was a scientist, and as such the first objection he made to his wife concerning this apparently compelling story was that it was nothing more than a hallucination due to lack of blood or triggered by fear of death. Then he heard the rest of the story.
It seems that the sister of Doris, Vida, had died only three weeks earlier. Since Doris was in such delicate condition, the death of her beloved sister was kept a secret from her. That is why the final part of her deathbed vision was so amazing to Barrett.

She spoke to her father, saying:

"I am coming," turning at the same time to look at me, saying, "Oh, he is so near."

On looking at the same place again, she said with a rather puzzled expression:

"He has Vida with him," turning again to me saying, "Vida is with him."

Then she said, "You do want me, Dad; I am coming."

Now, I ask you: Could all this have merely been wish fulfilment expressed in the form of a hallucination?

Well, that wouldn't explain why Doris saw Vida among the dead.

Exactly. Barrett himself considered such an explanation, but he rejected it because among the apparitions of the dead was someone whom Doris had not expected to see. Her sister, Vida, had died three weeks before. This explains why Doris was a bit surprised when she saw her sister.

What happened afterwards?

Like the Glasgow rapping for me, Doris' story aroused Sir William's curiosity, to the point that he embarked in a systematic study of what he named deathbed visions. You must understand that, like for NDEs, anecdotes of deathbed visions have appeared in literature and biographies throughout the ages. Barrett's, however, was the first attempt at documenting these phenomena. He painstakingly researched a large number of cases, checking all references and obtaining written, signed statements by witnesses and relatives whenever possible. In 1926 he published a summation of his findings in a book titled *Death Bed Visions*. In the many cases he studied, he discovered some interesting aspects of the experience that are not easily explained.

As in the case of Doris, it was not uncommon for the dying people who saw these visions to identify friends and relatives who they thought were still living. But in each case, according to Barrett, it was later discovered that these people were actually dead. You have to remember that communications then weren't what they are today, and it might take weeks or even months to learn that a friend or loved one had died. Barrett found it curious that children quite often expressed surprise that the "angels" they saw in their dying moments did not have wings. If the deathbed vision is just a hallucination, he thought, wouldn't a child see an angel as it is most often depicted in art and literature - with large, white wings?

Yes, all this is cute, but I need more "meat" to start thinking of another white fly.

Very good. Time then to meet two very interesting people. The first is Dr Karlis Osis Ph.D., a native of Riga, Latvia. He is one of the first psychologists to have obtained a doctorate degree with a thesis that dealt with extrasensory perception (University of Munich, 1950). As a Research Associate of the Parapsychology Laboratory at Duke University from 1951 to 1957, Dr. Osis was a colleague of Dr. J. B. Rhine (you remember the PSI experiments?). From 1962 to 1975, Dr. Osis was the Research Director for the American Society for Psychical Research. In that capacity, he conducted major cross-cultural surveys on ostensibly paranormal deathbed observations by physicians and nurses, which resulted in the publication of a book he co-authored, *At the Hour of Death* (New York: Hastings House, 1986).

The co-author of this landmark book is Dr. Erlendur Haraldsson Ph.D., a professor of psychology at the University of Iceland and visiting professor at the University of Virginia, and at the Institut für Grenzgebiete der Psychologie und Psychohygiene in Freiburg.
Osis and Haraldsson considered thousands of case studies and interviewed more than 1,000 doctors, nurses and others who attended the dying. This extraordinary work confirmed the findings of Sir William Barrett, but went also further by pointing to a number of fascinating consistencies:

- Belief in the afterlife or being religious appear to have no impact on the probability of experiencing a deathbed vision or on its content.

- Some dying people indeed report seeing angels and other religious or mythical figures. However, the vast majority report seeing members of the family or close friends who have previously passed away.

- Very often, the friends and relatives seen in these visions explicitly say that they have come to make the transition to the "other world" easier.

- The people having such visions are not scared. On the contrary, they generally feel reassured and experience great happiness. Those who were severely depressed or pain-ridden appear to be overcome with elation and momentarily relieved of pain. They appear quite willing to follow these apparitions, to go along with the transition.

- During the experience, people do not seem to be hallucinating or to be in an altered state of consciousness; rather, they appear to be quite aware of their real surroundings and conditions.

Yes, I must say this looks interesting. What kind of numbers are we talking about?

According to the information provided to Osis and Haraldsson by medical personnel only about ten per cent of people are conscious shortly before their death. Of this group one half to *two thirds have deathbed visions*.

That's a hell of a lot!

Yes, this indeed appears to be quite a widespread experience. Anyway, as we are talking numbers, did you know that 69% of Americans believe in the existence of angels?

No, but that does not surprise me... You remember what I was saying on the first day concerning the intellectually weak and the easily deluded? If you talk about angels I feel my scepticism raising up again.

I understand that. But stop and think for a moment. If you were raised in a religious environment and you happened to have an experience (deathbed vision, NDE or whatever) in which you saw what appears as heavenly, otherworldly creatures, how would you call them?

Yes – probably I would use the word angel.

OK. Now, let me digress slightly from the subject of deathbed visions and talk about angels. To do that, I would like to quote Dr. Melvin Morse, a paediatrician and neuroscientist best known for his seminal work on NDEs in children. In his book *Parting Visions* he writes:

Angels are reported under a variety of circumstances. Another account comes from Dr. Frank Oski, a professor of pediatrics under whom I trained at John Hopkins University. Oski is not a new-age guru. Rather he is a demanding pediatrician with an encyclopedic knowledge of medicine who insisted that his students come to the hospital having read the latest medical-journal articles. Yet to my great surprise Dr. Oski has been touched by the same mystical light described by people down through the ages who have had visions, including near-death experiences.

As a medical student Oski was enthusiastic about the potential of modern medicine, but frustrated by the fact that children die of congenital defects that are beyond anyone's control. One night he went to bed pondering the fate of a dying patient. Although he was doing his best, the child was not improving. He felt powerless to help and went to sleep wondering why this child had to die.

About an hour after falling asleep Oski was awakened by a bright light, one that shone in his room like a private sun. Oski could make out the form of a woman in the glow of the intense light. She had wings on her back and was approximately twenty years old. In a quiet and reassuring voice the woman explained to the speechless Oski why it was that children had to die.

"The angel (I don't know what else to call her) said that life is an endless cycle of improvements and that humans are not perfect yet. She said that most people have this secret revealed to them when they die, but that handicapped children often know this and endure their problems without complaining because they know that their burdens will pass. Some of these children, she said, have even been given the challenge of teaching the rest of us how to love. "'It stretches our own humanity to love a child who is less than perfect,' said the angel. 'And that is an important lesson for us.'"

Oski has been courageous enough to talk freely about his experience. He has even written about it for a major paediatric journal. In that article he wrote, "I will make no attempt to convince you as to the reality of my story. But I would merely ask that you keep an open mind on the mysteries of life which occur to you on a daily basis."

Day 7 - Out of Body Experiences

Today our talk will be a bit different. I've got a couple of pieces of very interesting evidence to share, but my main goal is to discuss with you the treacherous subject of human consciousness. To get started, let me ask you - where do you feel your consciousness is located?

Well, instinctively I would say in my head, somewhere behind my eyes.

Yes, that's what I would instinctively say too. In fact, that is what practically everybody says. Even with our eyes closed, probably out of habit, we identify the location of our consciousness with the vantage point from which we look out to the world. But then, if you experience an itch in one of your feet, or a pain in your stomach, where is your consciousness?

I think it would be too easy to say it is in my feet or in my stomach. In some way yes, but I also think consciousness is something different...

Yes, I agree. An itch or a pain is a sensation, but somehow we are aware of those sensations and of their location somewhere in our body. That awareness is consciousness, and, if you think of it, it is not really localized anywhere.

I agree, but... Why are we having this discussion?

Because Out of Body Experiences (OBEs), the subject of today's chat, provide us with some quite interesting insights on what consciousness might be, and further evidence of the nonlocal behaviour of which the human mind is apparently capable.

What do you mean with "what consciousness might be"? Consciousness is the activity of the brain - no brain, no consciousness.

No, no, no... Not that fast! The debate on the nature of consciousness is one of the liveliest in today's science and the least we can say is that there is no agreement, no definite conclusion.

But then, again, I know that so many psychological functions have been demonstrated to be linked to the activity of the neurons in our brain.

True and undisputed. If electromagnetic radiation of a certain wavelength hits the receptors in our retina, electric signals can be traced through the optic nerve up to the visual areas of the brain cortex, where certain neurons "light up". At that point, we say that we are seeing a color.

Exactly...

Yes, but we just agreed that consciousness is not equal to feeling a sensation or seeing a color. You can explain how the sensation arises, but you can't explain how, or why, we are *aware* of that sensation. How do you explain *how it feels* to see the colour blue?

Let me just tell you that His Holiness the Dalai Lama, who's always had a keen personal interested in science, has the habit of organizing every year gatherings of the world's top scientists in various disciplines. During these "Mind and Life" conferences, held in his Indian residence of Dharamsala, he learns about the most recent advances in such diverse fields as cosmology, evolutionary biology and neurosciences, and engages with the scientists in debates on the many amazing similarities and on the differences between modern science and traditional Buddhist teachings. Incidentally, he is famous, among other things, for having declared that "If the traditional teachings are in disagreement with the evidence provided by modern science, it means that our understanding of the teachings is incorrect".

Being a Buddhist supremely concerned with the human mind and how to transform it in order to improve our lives, it was only natural that His Holiness took a special interest in the question of consciousness and in the debate among neuroscientists. After several Mind and Life Conferences dedicated to this particular subject, his conclusion is that "currently, we do not have a comprehensive theory on the nature of consciousness".

But - come on... With all due respect for the opinions of the Dalai Lama - you've got about one hundred billion neurons wired together in an unimaginably complicated way, and you can see that psychological functions are associated with the activity of groups of those neurons. What else do you need? The brain is like a very powerful computer.

Yes, but are human mind and consciousness *entirely* dependent on the physical brain? Reductionist scientists say so, but others disagree. As top neurophysiologist Hunt said in 1995 "There is no neurophysiological research which conclusively shows that the higher levels of mind (intuition, insight, creativity, imagination, understanding, intent, decision, knowing) are located in brain tissue". The evidence arising from the psi experiments apparently indicates otherwise, not to mention the NDE evidence and the OBE experiences we'll discuss in a minute. I don't even want to start discussing the issue of survival now...

What other explanation may be there for consciousness, then?

Well, there are a few. Some scientists consider the involvement of quantum-level processes in the genesis of consciousness. Professor Richard Penrose has even proposed certain structures inside the neurons as the place where such large-scale quantum processes may take place. Since these structures are present even in very simple (and evolutionarily very old) organisms, Penrose says that consciousness is not a prerogative of humans alone, and provides quite some evidence for that.

Penrose the theoretical physicist?

Yes, very much him - the one who's worked many years with Stephen Hawking. You may read about his studies on consciousness in his classic *The Emperor's New Mind*.

There is another theory, though, which is considerably less developed but which I found absolutely fascinating. Put in very simple terms, it proposes that consciousness exists independently not only of the human brain, but of matter itself. Human brain then acts as a "receiver" that tunes into this field of consciousness and makes it available for living organisms.

Yes, I concede that that is truly fascinating. It is also utterly unbelievable, though.

Exactly like most of the evidence I am presenting to you... Anyway, I don't want to try to convince you of this - I'm not fully convinced myself. I just like the idea, and I like the fact that the theory is in accord with the findings of modern neurosciences, of parapsychology and psychic research, and with the esoteric knowledge gained by the mystics of all spiritual traditions.

Now you make me curious - how so?

Well, briefly then. Let's stick to the radio receiver example. Neuroscience says that certain neurons get activated when we perform certain functions. Exactly in the same manner, you can detect electric changes in the transistors of a radio receiver when it tunes in on a radio broadcast. Would you tell me that if the electromagnetic field produced by the radio broadcast was not there you would have sounds coming out of the speaker?

No, of course not.

So we agree that the electrical activity in the circuits is an essential part of the process of radio reception, but is not the process itself.

Yes, agreed.

Then perhaps the electric activity of the brain is instrumental in the raising of consciousness, but is not consciousness itself. Perhaps that activity may be associated with a consciousness field that exists outside and independently from the brain itself, like the electromagnetic field of a radio broadcast exists independently of the radio receiver.

Ummm... really interesting. Very far-fetched, but interesting indeed.

And, we could dwell on the equally interesting subject of the similarities between this theory and the core metaphysical teachings common to all religions. Spanning thousands of years of human history, mystics belonging to all the main spiritual traditions in different parts of the world have all told us the same thing: the universe in all its bewildering diversity emerges from one, single, undifferentiated source, and that source is conscious. Consciousness (the Divine consciousness in religious terms) *predates* matter and is responsible for its creation.

Wooow. You are totally losing me here!

I'm sorry, I'm sorry, you are completely right, I got carried away. Back to OBEs and to evidence, then. First of all, let's look at the phenomenon in general. OBEs are not at all a rare occurrence – in fact, they are surprisingly common. Different surveys have yielded somewhat different results, but estimates indicate that somewhere between five and ten percent of the general population reports having had at least one such experience. One of the reference studies in this field was conducted by Celia Elizabeth Green in 1967. She asked 380 students at Oxford University if they had had any experiences in which they felt themselves to be outside their body. As much as thirty-four per cent of the students replied affirmatively.

What does the experience consist of?

Well, that's why I started with this long introduction on consciousness and its location. OBEs are those curious and usually brief experiences in which a person's consciousness seems to leave the body so that s/he observes the world from a point of view other than that of the physical body, by means other than those of the physical senses. In most cases OBEers report seeing their own body, although, as in the case of the NDEs, the expression "seeing" is probably not the correct one.

Again, this looks pretty much like simple hallucinations.

Again, don't jump to conclusions so quickly. Let's look again at the results of the surveys. For starters, it seems that OBEs can occur to anyone in almost any circumstances: over 85 percent of those surveyed said they had had OBEs while they were resting, sleeping or dreaming, with only a small percentage occurring while the person is drugged or medicated. In addition - and this is very interesting - they can occur during almost any kind of activity. Green cites a couple of cases in which motor-cyclists, riding at speed, suddenly found themselves floating above their machines looking down on their own bodies still driving along. Accidents did not ensue. Airline pilots (perhaps affected by absence of vibration, and uniformity of sensory stimulation) have similarly found themselves apparently outside their aircraft struggling to get in.

This means that OBEs are not dreams either...

Well, that's a difficult one to answer. In fact, there are clear similarities between OBEs and dreams. In both we experience a world in which imagination plays a great part and we can perform feats not possible in everyday life. But the OBE differs in many important ways from ordinary dreams (we leave the discussion of so-called "lucid dreams" to a bit later). First, it usually occurs when the subject is awake – possibly drowsy or drugged, but not sleeping. Second, the imagery and activities of an OBE are usually much less bizarre and more coherent than those of an ordinary dream, and most often the scenery is based on the actual environment rather than the peculiar setting of dreams. Third, OBEers are adamant that their experience was nothing like a dream. Finally, there is a great difference in the state of consciousness: ordinary dreams are characterized by very cloudy consciousness at best, and are only recognized as dreams on waking up.

But, then, I know that you can train yourself to have what they call "lucid dreams".

Correct. You can indeed learn to acquire a good degree of consciousness during dreams: you are sleeping, you are dreaming, but you are aware that you are dreaming and you can exert some control on your dreamy experience. The boundary between OBEs and lucid dreams is indeed uncertain, and in fact some NDEers report that their experience began as a lucid dream. So, you may argue that the OBE is a kind of lucid dream occurring in the midst of waking life.

How can you tell them apart, then?

One way to find out is to determine the physiological state in which the OBE takes place. Catching an OBE in the laboratory may be difficult, as most people who have an OBE have only one, or at most a few, in a lifetime. You need a special kind of subject, one who is both able to induce an OBE at will, and willing to be subjected to the stress of being tested. Fortunately there are such subjects, and a number of researchers have carried out these experiments.

I don't want to bore you with the electrophysiology research details – I want to save time for something *way* more interesting. Let me just say that a) the start of an OBE does not appear to coincide with any abrupt physiological change (electroencephalogram or EEG, heartbeat, respiration, skin conductivity) and b) from the EEG point of view the OBE does not appear to occur in a state resembling dreaming.

Where does this leave us, then?

It leaves us still looking for evidence that the experience really takes place and is not simply an hallucination or a special kind of dream. Any suggestion?

From what I've learnt in the last few days, I would suggest trying to find out if OBEers can acquire "hidden" information – if they can learn something they could only learn if the consciousness somehow left the body.

Bravo! This is exactly what has been done. Already in 1972, for example, Janet Lee Mitchell, a researcher at the American Society for Psychical Research in New York, carried out a number of experiments with Ingo Swann, a known clairvoyant. During the experiments, different target objects were hidden on a platform suspended 3.5 metres above the floor of the room. After "projecting" his vision, Swann described the objects he saw both verbally and with illustrations. An independent judge correctly matched eight of Swann's drawings with the eight target objects used in the experiment.

The following year, Karlis Osis – whom we've already talked about yesterday - sent an open invitation throughout the United States to all individuals capable of projecting at will, to project themselves out of body and into the premises of the American Society for Psychical Research in New York. One hundred people were selected from the large number that volunteered. Four target objects were placed at a predetermined location within the building. Although the experiment didn't achieve total success, 15 per cent of the participants produced clear evidence of having visited the office through extraphysical means.

This is more like evidence for remote viewing, though.

Correct, and, although there are strong similarities, you may want to concentrate on controlled experiments on OBEs. Time then to meet another extraordinarily interesting guy.

Professor Charles Tart was born in 1937 and grew up in Trenton, New Jersey. He studied electrical engineering at the Massachusetts Institute of Technology before electing to become a psychologist. He received his doctoral degree in psychology from the University of North Carolina in 1963, and then received postdoctoral training in hypnosis research at Stanford University. He is currently a Core Faculty Member at the Institute of Transpersonal Psychology (Palo Alto, California) as well as Professor Emeritus of Psychology at the Davis campus of the University of California, where he served for 28 years.

Whilst investigating altered states of consciousness at Davis, Prof. Tart was fortunate enough to find a subject who claimed she could leave her body at will, and was available to be tested under laboratory conditions. The subject, mentioned in Prof. Tart's work as Miss Z for confidentiality reasons, agreed to spend four nights wired up to an electroencephalograph in the University's sleep laboratory. The goal of the experiment was – precisely as you said – to ascertain whether Miss Z could acquire information during her OBE. The information in question was a five digit number placed on top of a cabinet in the laboratory.

For the first three nights Miss Z reported having OBEs, but said she could not coordinate her movements enough to "go and read" what was written on a piece of paper on top of the cabinet. On the fourth night, however, she was able to do exactly that: she correctly reported that the number was 25132. This represents odds against chance of one in 100,000.

Couldn't she simply have woken up, read the number, and gone back to sleep?

Could Professor Tart be *so* stupid?

Well, yes – in fact it's stupid of me to ask. What controls were in place?

First, the only way she could have climbed on top of the cabinet (2.40 meters tall) was by stepping onto a chair or a stool. No such object was left in the laboratory. Second – and ultimately convincing – if she moved as much as 60 cm from her bed, the electrodes of the electroencephalograph would have been disconnected. Not only does the EEG not show any sign of disconnection, but also, at the time when Miss Z reported having her OBE, her alpha waves slowed by one and a half cycles per second. Tart had never seen anything like that before, and the unusual nature of the phenomenon was confirmed by one of his colleagues at Davis who was the world's leading expert on EEG rhythms during sleep.

This **is the kind of thing I like! And you seem to have plenty in stock, whatever we talk about…**

Thanks. In fact there is more. In recent years, a research project entitled Projective Field is being conducted by an independent group of researchers at the International Academy of Conscientology. The experiment, like previous ones, is aimed at understanding the processes by which an individual captures information through the OBE and remote viewing. Five batteries of well-designed experiments have already been conducted in Spain, Portugal, the United States and the United Kingdom. External auditors and judges participated in all experiments to attest to the validity of the scientific methodology. Intriguing preliminary results presented at the New York School of Medicine in 2002 showed that, of the 105 participants, 52 reported 93 instances of the OBE. The results presented also suggested that shapes of objects, followed by colours, are most easily perceived when outside the body. And.

Again, don't tell me there's more!

Yes. So far we have spoken of those OBEs in which the same person has the experience and reports it. There are in fact plenty of reports in which the OBEer was actually *seen by others* whilst out of body. A fairly typical example, collected during the extensive research carried out in the UK by Dr. Robert Crookall in the 1950's and 1960's, is the following:
I walked *through* my bedroom door and *through* my mother's door. She was sitting up in bed… with her head in her hands. I placed my hand on her head and said "Lie down – it's 2 a.m. and time you were asleep!" She said "Thank you son!" I returned to my bedroom, walking *through* the two doors. I saw my body in bed, and climbed back into my body. The next thing I knew I was sitting up in bed.

Now, you will understand that researchers wanted to see whether some kind of presence could be detected outside the body of the OBEer.

In 1979, in partnership with Donna L. McCormick and again at the American Society for Psychical Research in New York, Karlis Osis tested the kinetic effects of the projected consciousness. The team developed a means of measuring the presence of the extraphysical body of one projector (Alexander Tanous, in this experiment) through a system of sensors placed inside a sealed chamber. In addition, the projector was to attempt to perceive figures that were randomly produced by a specially designed optical system inside the chamber. Of the 197 attempts made by Tanous, 114 hits and 83 misses were made during 20 sessions. Every time that Tanous was able to correctly describe the figure selected and shown, *the sensors detected the presence of something inside the shielded chamber.*

Gosh. Impressive.

Definitely. And again, either we assume that two respected researchers and a well-established – and, as we will see in due course, *very* cautious and conservative – research Society conspired to create a phony experiment or...

Or we are looking at white fly number one million.

Right. Now, I want to take the last five minutes of your time to briefly mention another bit of research. Do you remember that in the beginning I said that "seeing" is probably not the right term to define perception during OBEs?

Yes.

And do you remember who investigated vision in the blind during Near-Death Experiences?

No. I remember the subject, but not the person.

That was Professor Kenneth Ring. I mention him again because he also investigated OBEs in the blind. Using the same methods that allowed him to identify subjects for his NDE research, he found a sample of ten people (four blind from birth, two adventitiously blind and four severely visually impaired) who reported OBEs. Nine out of ten in this group claimed to possess what seemed to be normal sight during the experience, and the reports of their sighted experiences were similar in important respects to those of the NDE group.

Did I manage to instil a doubt on the ultimate nature of human consciousness?

Day 8 - Mental mediumship today

I am absolutely convinced of the fact that those who once lived on earth can and do communicate with us. It is hardly possible to convey to the inexperienced an adequate idea of the strength and cumulative force of the evidence.

Sir William Barrett F.R.S.

We are now getting to the real core of the afterlife question. Let's start from scratch and define mediumship. What does a medium do?

I seem to remember that you said in the beginning that a medium is somebody who communicates with the deceased.

Excellent – that's it! More precisely, I would say that a medium is a channel of communication with the spirit world. No looking into the crystal ball to predict the future, no magic spells to win at the casino, no reading of the aura.

Yes, I understand that, but, as you can imagine, I have big problems with the very idea of a "spirit world".

Oh, yes, I can understand that very well. Still today, after all I've learnt, I still find myself slipping back into doubt at times. All this, all we are talking about, all the different pieces of evidence point to something that is so exquisitely unbelievable that there are times when I say to myself that there *must* be an explanation, something less unbelievable than human personality surviving physical death. But then another piece of evidence comes my way, and I study it, and I ask myself questions, and most times I find myself staring at yet another white fly. In some cases, there may be a few possible alternative explanations, but they look so outlandish that in comparison the existence of an afterlife actually makes sense...

I see what you mean, but I still feel that I have to come across these particular white flies myself. For the time being I remain convinced that mediums are fakes. They may be convinced themselves of what they do, they may believe in it, or they may be just plain fraudsters – the substance doesn't change. And, the entire thing works because we are all afraid of death, we all *want* an afterlife to exist and we are ready to believe anything that goes in that direction.

These are very sensible ideas. In fact, anybody who's ever considered the subject of mediumship – or, more generally, of the existence of an afterlife – has mulled over these ideas. I don't want to propose any answer now. As we have been doing since the beginning, I will stick to presenting the evidence, and you will draw your conclusions yourself.

To understand what mental mediumship is all about, I see no better way than to look at one story involving Gordon Smith, considered Britain's most accurate medium today. I particularly like Gordon, not only because of his astonishing gift, but – and perhaps mainly – for his adorable, low key, humorous personality. He embodies the quintessence of the real medium, in as all he does is done out of compassion and with the aim of relieving the suffering of people who have lost a loved one. Although he has become a bit of a world celebrity and is an established TV and printed media personality in the UK, he keeps making his living by cutting hair in his native Glasgow. "The Psychic Barber", as he is sometimes known, *never* asks for money for his private sittings. Here is the story, as told by Gordon himself in his book *The Unbelievable Truth* (Hay House, 2005).

What does it mean to be a medium? What do I actually do? It is not always easy to explain. Saying that I communicate with disincarnate spirits who have gone on after physical death seems strange to some people. What sort of messages are passed on? What convinces people that their loved ones really are communicating with them? I've often thought that a good way to explain the process would be to film someone before they came to see me and ask them to share their story and what they hoped to gain from the encounter.

In January 2004, that very thing happened during the filming of a BBC documentary in which a couple who had lost their son in a car accident the year before were brought to see me. The director of the film had not allowed me to have any prior knowledge of the couple at all, not even where they were being brought from. This should actually be standard practice, as the less the medium knows about a person, the more convincing the evidence they may receive from the spirit world. In this case, unknown to me the couple had been filmed for some time before our meeting.

On a cold February morning, I was waiting in the library of the London Spiritual Mission, where the sitting was to take place. This is one of the most beautiful Spiritualist churches in the UK, where mediums from all over the country come to demonstrate their skills. Once the film crew decided they were ready to begin, a couple who I would imagine were in their forties were asked to sit opposite me and I explained to them how the sitting would proceed. Normally, I 'tune into' the spirit world by asking the spirit people if they would like to come and contact their loved one, but this time, even as I began to tell the couple how it may work, I could hear the voice of a young man shouting the name 'Andrew' over and over in my ear. With this I knew I had a communicator from the spirit world.

I started by saying, 'There is a young man on the other side and he is asking for Andrew'. Immediately the man answered 'I'm Andrew'. Then I heard another name. I turned to the woman and said, 'You must be Margareta'. 'No,' she answered, but then it changed and I told her, 'I'm sorry, he has changed it to Greta'. This time she smiled and said that was her name.

Their son was now communicating at high speed, often so fast that I had to slow him down, but this was characteristic of how he behaved in life, so his mother told me. He told me that his name was Nige, short for Nigel, and that he and his friend were together in the spirit world as they had been both involved in the same accident. He went on to ask after other family members, told me to tell his sister to go back to her studies and mentioned a Mr. Trainer, who turned out to be a tutor at college. Then he asked me to mention Ilkley. This is where he had been brought up and where he had spent much of his time with his teenage friends.

Nige wanted to convince his family that he was still very much part of their life. He asked me to ask his father why no one was wearing his watch, which was at home in a blue box. His father said he wanted to, but hadn't got around to putting in the new battery that it needed. Then Nige told his mother that he had been with her that morning when she had picked up three letters from behind the front door and he knew she had wanted to bring the large picture of him to the sitting, touched his face and put it back. He also said that she could feel his presence when she walked through the lane at the back of her house. All this was accepted by Andrew and Greta.

Nige also asked me to tell them that he had been with them when they had gone to Ilkley Moor and stood on their favourite large rock. The camera and sound men were shocked at this, as they had filmed the family walking on Ilkley Moor the previous day and Andrew had stood on his son's favourite rock and said that he would say that it was like standing on the top of the world. At the close of the sitting the crew got again a bit spooked when young Nige asked me to tell them all that he and his friend were fine and he really was standing on top of the world.

Afterwards Greta and Andrew told me how moved and uplifted they had been by the sitting. They felt that their son's personality had really shone through and their overwhelming impression had been that he really was communicating with them. They were absolutely amazed that his spirit had been with them when they had been filmed on the moors and that he had then been able to tell them about it through my mediumship.

Is this all on film?

Most definitely, exactly as recounted by Gordon.

Was it aired on television?

Yes, of course, it was on BBC 4.

Well, I must admit that this makes the case for fraud very little credible.

Thank you very much for saying this. This is the same conclusion I would draw. Now, can you think of any alternative explanation – I mean alternative to the fact that the disincarnate spirit of the boy was actually communicating with his parents?

The main problem I have with this story is the apparent level of detail in the information provided. I always believed that mediums would tell

people very generic things, a little like the horoscopes you read in the newspapers. Anybody can recognize a grain of truth in the nonsense you read there. Bereaved parents would zoom in on such grains and make them into big boulders to satisfy their need to believe that their loved one has somehow survived death. But in the case...

...in the case of Gordon Smith, it's the UK daily newspaper *Daily Mail* that says "There is nothing ambiguous about the messages Gordon conveys".

Is he really exceptional?

Mediumship of this level is actually quite rare. Hundreds of mediums demonstrate every week in Spiritualist churches around the world, with varying degrees of ability. What is extraordinary in mediums like Gordon is not only the level of accuracy, but the incredible consistency – one church service after another, one private sitting after another, year after year. However, when you start considering the ocean – truly, an ocean – of evidence collected during the last 150 years in this field, you realize that very high-level mental mediumship is rare, but not exceptional. Here's another example, a small fragment from the verbatim transcription of a taped sitting with medium Stewart Lawson. Please appreciate that these are not isolated pieces of information amidst a stream of irrelevant statements, but a continual flow. In brackets we find the comments by the sitter.

Stewart:- Your father is here. He greets you. I sense a dog that has just followed your father and is near to him; I can't see it yet. The dog barked! Suddenly there was a bark of a dog. I still can't see it so I can't describe it. But from its bark, it was not a wee dog [Our dog, who had died shortly before my father, was a large Labrador].

I can see it now. It is a Labrador [Correct].

He wasn't black - he was golden [Correct].

The dog is very close to your father [My father used to look after him, and deal with all that was related to trying to stop his health deteriorating. In the year before they both died, they became very attached].

The dog passed over before him [Correct].

Only a short period before him [Correct - ten days].

It was a dog and not a bitch as I can hear what your father is calling him [Correct. I then ask what my father is calling him]. He is saying 'Ben! Sit down!' [Correct - this being the dog's name. At this point the medium's voice and mannerisms become like my father's].

Yes, the dog has now come into vision - he is a large golden Labrador and he's now laid down by your father's feet. Your father is saying 'Look! He's OK now'. He is stroking and pointing to his back. He keeps pointing to his back and saying 'He's fine now'. Was there something wrong that was connected to back? This seems to be the cause of his passing [Correct. The dog suffered a severe skin allergy that was far worse on his back than anywhere else and this eventually resulted in him being put to 'sleep' because he was in so much discomfort].

Now, can I bring you back to possible alternative explanations?

Well, I think... I think I've even seen on TV that skilled people can extract information by talking all the time, saying a lot of generic things and interpreting the body language of the sitters to understand if they've got anything correct. If they feel that they hit something, they can build on that until they arrive at something significant.

This is technically called "fishing" (the talking all the time in generic terms) and "cold reading" (looking for signs that some of the generic statements is correct, and building on that). By looking back at the two examples we've just considered (Gordon Smith and Stewart Lawson), do you see any trace of fishing or cold reading?

No, in effect those looked like a continuous stream of communication. Very specific information being given, no uncertainties, no asking. It can't be all the time like that, though...

Of course it isn't: there's plenty of cold readers around – only, they're not mediums! There are a lot of skilled mentalist magicians, some honestly making a living in the entertainment business, and others just taking advantage of other people. Now, consider this: nobody, I mean *not one single cold reader* has ever accepted to be tested under the same strictly controlled conditions used to test mediums in universities and psychic research centers. Speaking of which, there is another interesting story involving skeptics...

Not Ray Hyman again!

Oh, yeeeees! This is the third example of a major research project that our friend tried unsuccessfully to debunk. Three different and completely unrelated projects, and the same advocate for the hard-nosed skeptics: you may start to wonder who's really getting some notoriety by playing the devil's advocate...

The story revolves around Professor Gary Schwartz, initially an assistant professor at Harvard and then a psychology professor at Yale University for 12 years and the author of over 400 scientific papers. Schwartz has long been interested in the possible survival of consciousness after death. In a very interesting book (*The afterlife experiments*, Atria, 2002), he reports on his and fellow psychologist Linda Russek's experiments to determine whether consciousness survives death. The results of the experiments, carried out at the Human Energy Systems Laboratory of the University of Arizona, showed definite examples of precognition and surprisingly accurate observations by the mediums by using single, double and even triple blind protocols. There is, by the way, an excellent scientific paper that describes such protocols. It is unfortunately also very technical, but it makes incredibly interesting reading. It's called *Methodological Advances in Laboratory Based Mediumship Research*, by Julie Beischel, PhD and Gary E. Schwartz, PhD and is available online on the University of Arizona website.

We don't want to dwell on the results here – we are discussing possible alternative explanations, and in particular cold reading. At some early stage in the experiments, before blind protocols were employed, in order to address the criticism by the skeptics Prof. Schwartz convened a two day meeting including highly experienced professional mentalist magicians and cold readers, and Ray Hyman. Most of the experts agreed that they could not apply their conventional mentalist tricks under the strict experimental conditions (no knowledge of the sitter's identity, and no verbal or non-verbal visual or auditory cues/feedback). However, a vocal subset (Hyman being one of the three), made the claim that if they had a year or two to practice, they might be able to figure out a way how to fake what the mediums were doing under these experimental conditions. Gary Schwartz says:

"My response to this vocal subset was simple. It was "show me." Just as I don't take the claims of the mediums on faith, I don't take the claims of the magicians on faith either. Mentalist magicians who make these claims will have to sit in the research chair and show us that they can do what they claim they can do. Thus far, the few cold readers who have made these extreme claims have refused to be experimentally tested."

Funny – isn't it? The skeptics refusing to use the same scientific method they advocate.

Exactly! Anyway, the possible explanation of cold reading is excluded not only by the multiple-blind protocols used in recent years, but also by a technique used as far back as the beginning of last century – proxy sitting.

Proxy sitting?

A proxy sitting is a sitting in which the medium interacts with one subject who is *not* the person related to the deceased relative. In this protocol, one John shows up for a sitting and asks to communicate with the disincarnate spirit of one George, born on such and such day and dead on such and such day, saying that he was his father. Unknown to the medium, George was not John's father – John is a proxy sitter. The medium gets in touch with the spirit of George and provides information to John, who writes it down on a piece of paper. After the sitting, the information is shown to Jack, the real son of George, who rates it for accuracy.

And it works?

Yes, it does. I don't want to annoy you with lengthy transcripts from innumerable experiments. Take my word - you basically get the same accuracy as in normal sittings.

Before we continue, let me ask: were the experiments of Prof. Schwartz ever replicated?

Certainly. And here I would like to introduce you to another eminent – and eminently adorable – personality in this field, somebody whom we will encounter again when looking at other subjects in the course of our discussion. Archie Roy is a Professor Emeritus of Astronomy in the University of Glasgow, a Fellow of the Royal Society of Edinburgh, The Royal Astronomical Society and the British Interplanetary Society. He has published 20 books, some 70 scientific papers and scores of articles, and directed NATO's Advanced Scientific Institute.

For the best part of thirty years he has also been passionately interested in psychical research and helped to found PRISM (Psychical Research Involving Selected Mediums) which encourages, guides and funds research work with mediums. The papers published by the PRISM program validate mediumship showing effects with odds against chance of ten billion to one.

Wow...

Now, any other possible explanations?

I was thinking about telepathy. Could the medium be acquiring information directly from the sitter's mind?

Excellent! On your own, you have come up with the two explanations – cold reading and psi – that have been proposed by experts since the beginning of the investigations on mediumship. Unfortunately, a number of reasons force us to rule out the psi hypothesis. Let's examine them briefly.

Number one: as we have said when discussing the evidence for telepathy, the size of the effect is small. People can indeed acquire information from other people's minds when all known sensory channels are unavailable, but the level of detail of such information is nowhere near that communicated by mental mediums.
Number two: the mind reading hypothesis does not explain the results of the proxy sittings. The real sitter is not present at the sitting, and the medium doesn't even know who the real sitter is.

Number three: the mind reading hypothesis explains even less the results of the multiple-blind experiments.

Number four: way before modern scientific protocols were employed, one single thing excluded the mind reading hypothesis and provided to many the most direct proof that communications received from the spirit world indeed come from disincarnate personalities – the fact that such communications often contain information which is *unknown even to the sitter*.

Now, the last bit is extremely important, and I would like to spend some time on it. To do that, we have to move out of the laboratories and to enter the "field". It is a major turning point in our discussion: from now on, as we move from subject to subject, we will talk mostly about anecdotal evidence.

This is not scientific, then...

No, that's wrong. The debate about what constitutes "real science" and what doesn't has been raging for centuries, and once you start scratching the surface you immediately understand that what we call "science" goes well beyond laboratory tests under controlled conditions. Let's say, for example, that a biologist goes to Antarctica to study one particular aspect of the penguins' behaviour. After five weeks of observation he comes back with a report saying that the penguins do this and that. Is that not science?

Well, of course it is. But we expect that if another biologist went and observed the same penguins, he would report the same behaviour.

Precisely. And this is precisely what happens with most of the anecdotal evidence I am talking about. People observe phenomena and report what they have seen. And then other people observe the same phenomena and report the same kind of things. Just swap the biologist with a psychic researcher and the penguins with mediums or other psychic phenomena.
Then there are personal accounts. Granted – people tell all sort of things. But when a lot, really a lot, of people all tell the same kind of stories, and the stories coming from totally unrelated people are so consistent, when they all fit like pieces of the same puzzle, and fit with the laboratory data and with the field research, then...

Then – you are going to say – you are looking at a *huge* white fly!

Now, look who's the one reading my mind! You perfectly got my point.

I'm getting good at this!

Just one more important thing: over the next few days, I will give you some pretty interesting examples of various increasingly inexplicable phenomena (I mean inexplicable if you don't accept that human personality survives physical death). Please remember that these examples are just a fraction (I would say less than ten percent) of the examples I have personally read about. And what I have read is a tiny fraction (certainly less than one percent) of what is available in the literature. Think of the thousands of scientific papers, newspaper articles, media reports, of the hundreds of books available in many languages, not to talk about the myriad of personal accounts that are told and recorded in a way or another. Beyond any specific example, as striking as it may be, try to see the one hundred similar examples that I am not going to tell you about but are there nevertheless. At any moment, try to reflect on the phenomenal weight of the evidence.

Now, I promised you an interesting anecdote about information mediums sometime provide which is not known to the sitter. What should be your automatic reflex as I tell this story?

To think that there are many more similar stories. I believe you are going to use this just as an example.

Excellent! Thank you very much. This particular story also comes from Glasgow, Scotland, and features possibly the most formidable medium the UK has seen during the last part of the 20th century. Albert Best worked as a postman all of his life, and despite being a prime star in the firmament of mediums (or, more likely, just because of that...) he was universally described as the most humble, compassionate and caring individual. Albert Best, who was a close friend and in many ways a mentor for Gordon Smith, whom we met at the beginning of your conversation on mediums, comes into play a little later in the story.

First you have to learn about Rev. David Kennedy, a Church of Scotland minister, and his wife Ann, who died in her forties from an incurable disease. During the last days of her life, Ann insisted with Rev. Kennedy that she would find a way to come back and communicate with him. At the time, Rev. Kennedy acknowledged this out of love for her, although the concept of an afterlife from which spirit people could communicate was against his faith.

We understand that the death of his beloved wife tried the Reverend to the extreme. In the midst of a nearly full blown clinical depression, remembering the vow she he had made on her deathbed, at some stage he went to see a Spiritualist medium called Lexie Findletter. She gave him a message from a woman called Ann who claimed to be his wife, but David's skepticism and religious conditioning didn't allow him to accept it. David says, however, that as he was leaving the room Lexie told him "Your wife is determined to communicate with you and she'll find a way". About a week later, we find David feeling even worse, also tormented by the thought of not having given the spirit of his wife a real chance to communicate. At some stage, he says out loud to the empty room "Come on, Ann, give me a sign, something that no one could possibly know, please". Picture him as he collapses to the sofa, terminally sad and worried about the sermon he would have to prepare for his service later in the day, and dozes off.

Next thing he knows is that the phone is ringing loudly. He jumps up from the sofa, realizing he's got just five minutes to prepare the sermon and find a clean minister's collar. He fumbles around the room looking for old notes and he can't remember where his collars are. Meanwhile, the phone keeps ringing. After what seems like an eternity, and still not having found what he was looking for, he picks up the phone and answers angrily, 'Can I help you?'.

'Your wife Ann is with me', says a voice. 'She tells me that your clean collars are in the bottom drawer of your wardrobe and the speech you prepared last year for this service is in the top drawer of your desk. Incidentally, my name is Albert Best. Goodbye.'

Now, put yourself in the shoes of David Kennedy. He remembers meeting Albert Best with his wife, years before, at a social gathering, and that people raved about him. He also remembers that, on that occasion, Albert had told Ann that her brother who had died during the Second World War was standing beside her, and provided a perfect description of him. But how did Albert Best know to phone at that moment with the exact information he needed? And how did he get the number?

That is really incredible!

Wait – the best is still to come. That particular day, after having found the items he was looking for exactly where described by Albert, David went on about his business as well as he could. During the following weeks, David then made contact with Albert to understand what was going on. Albert explained that Ann had appeared to him in spirit form and provided information about the collar and the sermon. After a few meetings, the two men understand that there is a pattern at work: if David sent out a thought to Ann as he was alone in the house, within a short time Ann would appear to Albert and he would be on the phone to David. Things even got nearly out of control, as Albert was once quoted saying, "Tell your wife to stop bloomin' bothering me, it's the middle of the night!".

This thing went on for over a year, and Albert confided to Gordon Smith (who tells this story in his already mentioned book *The Unbelievable Truth*) to be annoyed with Ann's frequent requests for him to call her husband. Albert, however, knew that until Rev. Kennedy would have been convinced that his wife went on living in the spirit world, these communications would have continued.

And here we come to the point of the proof. You remember that we spoke about mediums providing information that not even the sitter is aware of, and that being an almost definitive proof of personality survival?

Yes I do.

Well, that's exactly what happened at the end of our Glasgow story. David Kennedy, as we know already, could not accept the idea of messages from the other side because of his faith. However, the longer the communications went on, the more baffled he became. At some point, he made a request to his wife: she should provide a piece of information that he himself was not aware of – something he would have been able to confirm with a member of the family. If that information came, he would have finally accepted the idea of her survival.

The next time Ann appeared to Albert, she told him to tell her husband to call her sister and ask about the ballet shoes. When David did so, his sister in law was astonished that he knew of the private joke that had been a secret between her and her sister for many years.

After much thought and investigation into his experiences, Rev. Kennedy decided to write his story, which later became a book called *A Venture into Immortality*.

Day 9 - Mental mediumship in the past

I regard the existence of discarnate spirits as scientifically proved and I no longer refer to the skeptic as having any right to speak on the subject. Any man who does not accept the existence of discarnate spirits and the proof of it is either ignorant or a moral coward. I give him short shrift, and do not propose any longer to argue with him on the supposition that he knows anything about the subject.

James Hyslop

Gosh - the quote is extremely explicit... Who is James Hyslop?

James Hyslop has been a Professor of Logic and Ethics from 1889-1902 at Columbia University, New York. He was described as "a most obdurate closed-minded skeptic who for many years disseminated much anti-psychic propaganda".

Well, the quote doesn't seem very skeptical to me!

Yes, you are right. Prof. Hyslop was forced to change his mind after investigating one of the most outstanding mental mediums who ever lived - Mrs. Leonore Piper from Boston. During the séances he attended, messages from his father and relatives poured through, reminding him of facts known and unknown to him. He was immensely puzzled, and was eventually forced by the evidence to concede. On a particular occasion, the sixteenth sitting of his investigation, he was able to verify no fewer than 152 out of the 250 incidents mentioned by Mrs. Piper.

I know what you are about to say...

What?

That this is only one example among so many, and so on and so forth...

Ha! Yes – you make me laugh! In fact, I was not planning to say that just now, but you are very right. I am faced with the same dilemma all the time: an extraordinary amount of information, and only a limited amount of time – not to mention your patience...

So we are focusing on a few examples, right?

Yes, very right. I will tell you just three stories that I believe are very representative of the "historical" aspects of mental mediumship. We will talk about famous mediums, famous scientists, attempted debunking and even a court case that made a sensation in Britain during World War II.

And we begin with?

We begin with Mrs. Piper herself, and with the arduous attempts to prove that she was a fake.

But Ray Hyman was not even born back then!

No, he wasn't, but skeptics abounded even during the decades in which "spiritism" (as it was then called) enjoyed the highest popularity in the UK and the US. In fact, this story has an interesting angle, as the arch-skeptic in question was under the mandate of the Society for Psychical Research.

Society for Psychical Research? I think you already mentioned it. What is it? And – come to think of it – should they not be the first ones to support the claims of mediums?

OK – let's first turn again to Wikipedia:

The Society for Psychical Research (SPR) is a non-profit organization which started in the United Kingdom and later acquired branches in other countries. Its stated purpose is to understand "events and abilities commonly described as psychic or paranormal by promoting and supporting important research in this area" and to "examine allegedly paranormal phenomena in a scientific and unbiased way."

It was founded in 1882 by a group of eminent thinkers including Edmund Gurney, Frederic Myers, William Barrett, Henry Sidgwick, and Edmund Dawson Rogers. The Society's headquarters are today in Marloes Road, London. Part of the extensive library and archive it has built over the years is held at the University of Cambridge.

It publishes the quarterly, peer-reviewed *Journal of the Society for Psychical Research*, the irregular *Proceedings* and the magazine *Paranormal Review*. It holds an annual conference, regular lectures and two study days per year. Its French branch, the French Society for Psychical Research, publishes the *Journale de la Société Française pour Recherche Psychique*. Its American counterpart, the American Society for Psychical Research, publishes the *Journal of the American Society for Psychical Research*. After the French branch of the Society was formed, the Society as a whole became known as the International Society for Psychical Research (ISPR).

Heavy stuff, then.

Very. And "very establishment"... The last president of the Society, until 2004, was Bernard J. Carr, professor of mathematics and astronomy at Queen Mary, University of London. The current president is John Poynton, Professor Emeritus of biology and research associate of the Natural History Museum in London.

You mean an "old boys club"?

Yes, in a way... The thing, you see, is that the SPR has traditionally been extremely cautious on – not to say opposed to – the issue of survival of human personality beyond physical death. It does consider it (and it even has a Survival Committee), but has always been very demanding in terms of evidence. Now you can understand why, during the last years of the 19th century, the Society appointed a very senior and widely respected member, Richard Hodgson, to investigate Leonore Piper with the almost explicit aim of showing that she was a fake.

Interesting. What happened, then?

As you would expect, Hodgson was firmly determined to expose Mrs. Piper. In order to avoid her getting in touch with prospective sitters before the séances, he engaged private investigators to follow her, to report on whom she met outside her home, to intercept her mail. He invited negative "dummy" sitters unknown to anyone to her sittings. She was even taken to England where she knew no one and it was arranged for her to stay with members of the British SPR where she could be constantly monitored.

Despite all these measures, Mrs. Piper would regularly go into a trance, then what is called a "control" – an intelligence from the afterlife, who, in the case of Mrs. Piper, was known by the name of Dr. Phinuit – would take over and start to give a great deal of accurate information and messages from those who had passed on.

Hodgson was growing increasingly frustrated, and somehow appeared to have lost his emotional balance. At some stage he even wrote:

"... I can't prove anything at all ... I can't prove fraud, I can't prove cheating, I can't prove trickery against Mrs. Piper but trust me; don't believe anybody else except me; just believe me because only I have the truth about these things but no one else has".

Then, things were to take a dramatic turn with the sudden death of George Pellew, one of Richard Hodgson's own friends. To everybody's astonishment, George Pellew, appeared shortly thereafter as the control of Mrs. Piper in place of Dr. Pinhuit. Hodgson was now in a unique position to ask his dead friend thousands of questions about their relationship: Mrs. Piper – or more correctly George Pellew speaking through her – kept answering his thousands of questions correctly.

Over several months Hodgson introduced over 150 sitters at séances to the entranced Mrs. Piper. Thirty of these had known George Pellew while he was alive, the others had never met him. George Pellew was able to correctly identify all of the sitters whom he had known. Most of them sat and talked and reminisced with George Pellew, speaking through Mrs. Piper, as if he himself was there in the flesh. His only mistake was to fail to identify a person whom he had not met since the person was a very small girl!

These meetings were so absolutely impressive that Richard Hodgson wrote his report explaining in detail why he was wrong in his earlier reports and that now he had irretrievably accepted the existence of the afterlife. He claimed that he had communicated with intelligences from the afterlife and he couldn't wait to get there himself.

"...at the present time I cannot profess to have any doubt but that the chief 'communicators' to whom I have referred in the foregoing pages, are veritably the personalities that they claim to be, that they have survived the change we call death, and that they have directly communicated with us whom we call living, through Mrs. Piper's entranced organism." (SPR Proceedings Vol 13, 1898, H 10)

I must give it to you – you never fail to entertain me with these stories.

It's great fun, isn't it? But do I make you think as well? Please, take a minute and reconsider the story you've just heard. The story is not invented – there are masses of documents to prove it. Can the hundreds of people involved in Hodgson's investigation *all* be wrong or deluded? Can this be a gigantic conspiracy? If Hodgson were to have lost it and "gone cuckoo", how do you explain the fact the George Pellew showed up as Mrs. Piper's control shortly after his death? And, even more to the point, how do you explain that two previous major investigations (led by Professor William James of Harvard University and by the very Prof. Hyslop we mentioned at the beginning) had come exactly to the same conclusions?

The second story is about another top UK scientist of the beginning of the last century. Sir Oliver Lodge obtained a Bachelor of Science degree from the University of London in 1875. He was appointed professor of physics and mathematics at University College, Liverpool, at the young age of 30. He then received the Doctor of Science degree in 1887 and in 1900 he moved from Liverpool back to the Midlands to become the first Principal of the new Birmingham University, remaining there until his retirement in 1919.

Sir Oliver too somehow crossed paths with Mrs. Piper. He had started researching mediums in 1883 and got to meet Mrs. Piper when was she was being tested in England by the SPR. These séances were a true revelation for him: he received a number of messages from deceased loved ones that convinced him that personality survives physical death. Already in 1890, Sir Oliver was publishing detailed accounts of his findings. His convictions were to grow even stronger after the death of two close friends and associates, Frederick Myers and Edmund Gurney, who were to communicate incredibly detailed evidence through Mrs. Piper.

What really stands out in Sir Oliver's story, however, is a series of remarkable communications that he received through different mediums from his son, Raymond, who was killed in the First World War on September 14th, 1915. Now, follow me closely as I tell you about one particular episode.

On November 25th, 1915, Sir Oliver received a letter from a complete stranger, who said that she had a photograph of Raymond with the officers of the South Lancashire Regiment taken just before he died. She offered to send it to the Lodges and they gratefully accepted the offer.

On December 3rd, 1915, Sir Oliver had a sitting with Gladys Osborne Leonard, a celebrated trance medium. In that occasion, Raymond gave a complete description of this photograph that neither the medium nor the Lodges had yet seen. He described himself as sitting on the ground, with a fellow officer placing his hand on Raymond's shoulder.

On December 7 1915, the photograph arrived and, to the complete astonishment of the Lodgess, it matched perfectly the description given by Raymond through the medium four days earlier. Many other messages came forward from Raymond, all of which were very evidential to the Lodge. This first hand testimony by a reputable scientist was published in Sir Oliver Lodge's 1916 book *Raymond or Life After Death*.

Well... what can I say?

You don't have to say anything. Just reflect again, as either you refuse all this *in toto* – I mean you decide to believe that the Principal of Birmingham University invented this entire story and published it in a book at the very peak of his academic career – or you are left with just one possible explanation: that human personality somehow survives physical death.

I would like to end my short review of "historical" mediumship with the tale of Helen Duncan and of the nationwide clamor that surrounded her court trial in 1944. Before we get into the story, however, let me tell you that we'll be talking about a materialization medium this time.

A "materialization" medium?

Yes, that's correct. We will talk about that in detail in a couple of days, and then I will share with you my own difficulties with this particular subject. For the time being, let me just tell you that materialization, in psychic terms, is "the claimed manifestation of temporary, more or less organized, apparitions in varying degrees of form, often possessing human physical characteristics and said to be shaped for a temporary existence from a substance called ectoplasm". All that is not important for this particular story, however, as we are mostly concerned with Mrs. Duncan's mental mediumship, that is the capacity of conveying messages from the spirit world which are completely beyond the knowledge of the medium and even of the very sitters attending séances.

Helen Duncan was born in 1897 in Callander, a small Scottish town, the daughter of a master cabinet maker. Her family was far from rich, and she struggled to earn a living even after her marriage at the age of 20. To sustain this large family and a disabled husband she worked in the local bleach factory by day, and then went on to attend her Spiritual work and domestic duties by night. She would make a small amount of cash from her sittings, mostly token donations from friends and neighbours, and often discretely use it to pay the local doctor for those patients who were destitute.

The main reason for Helen's spectacular rise in popularity was her rare psychic gift of being a vehicle for physical phenomena whilst in trance state: dead loved ones were reported to appear in physical form, to speak and to touch their earthly relatives and in this way bring both proof of survival and much comfort to thousands of traumatised and grieving wartime families. By the 1930s and 1940s she was travelling the length of wartime Britain giving regular séances in hundreds of Spiritualist churches and home circles. The evidence that flowed from these physical phenomena séances was reportedly astonishing.

The story which made Helen Duncan a national celebrity can be traced back to one night in May 1941, at the time when she was in living Portsmouth, the home of the Royal Navy. That particular night, whilst Helen was in trance, she passed on the news that a British battleship had sunk. It so happens that among the sitters there was one Brigadier R. C. Firebrace, who took note of this piece of information and learnt shortly afterwards that HMS Hood had sunk that day with a loss of 1,100 lives. A committed military man and a patriot, Firebrace felt that he had to report these facts to the Intelligence Agencies, who immediately took an interest in Helen Duncan's activities.

The crucial episode of the story was to take place a few months later, when, at one of Helen's séances, the spirit of a sailor appeared before his mother. He materialised in full uniform with an inscription on his cap, HMS Barham. He stated that his ship had been sunk in action. This was not unusual at Helen Duncan's séances, as the war produced numerous dead sailors and many of the sitters were sailors' relatives.

After a few days, *Psychic News* editor Maurice Barbanel, who had attended the séance, telephoned the British Admiralty requesting confirmation of the sinking and enquiring why they had not informed the mother that her son was dead at sea. This was to cause a major stir: *the sinking of HMS Barnham was considered 'Top Secret' information and British Military Intelligence was appalled that there had been a leak.* They had held back on the announcement fearing the loss of 861 seamen, torpedoed by a German U-boat, was bad for public morale. At the time, the British government denied the vessel had gone down, and the British War Office had no official news. It was only months later the Barnham was indeed reported lost in an enemy attack.

These facts left many observers disconcerted: how to explain the materialization of the sailor's spirit, instantly recognized by his own mother, and, especially, how to explain the fact that the spirit communicated secret information which was to be released only months after?

Some circles, however, reacted not with puzzlement but with open suspicion. The British Military Intelligence started seriously suspecting that Helen Duncan was a spy, and began monitoring her activity discretely but with increasing attention. A naval officer in plain clothes was sent to regularly attend the séances and report to the Admiralty. Things escalated to the point that, in the climate of paranoia preceding D-Day in 1944, they became concerned that Helen Duncan was a threat to national security. The decision was finally taken that Helen was somehow to be silenced.

The drama reached a climax on January 19th, 1944, when a plainclothes policemen and a naval lieutenant were sent to a séance to gather evidence of fraud and arrest the medium. As usual, that evening Helen went into trance and started to materialize ectoplasm. At that point the policeman jumped out of his chair blowing his whistle and, expecting the ectoplasm to be a white sheet, he made a grab for it. The spirit, however, instantly dematerialized. To the great frustration of the officers, after a thorough search nothing could be found to implicate fraud, no sheet, no false beards, no rubber gloves, no accomplice. Nevertheless, Helen was formally arrested with three members of the audience.

The legal proceedings which ensued were nothing short of baffling. The original charge laid against Helen by the Portsmouth Magistrates was that of Vagrancy, which would be a five shilling fine. However, Helen was refused bail and sent to Holloway prison for four days. The alleged crime was then changed to conspiracy: a hanging offence. By the time the case came before the judge at the Old Bailey, it was once again altered. The defendants were now accused of contravening the Witchcraft Act of 1735. Bail was refused again (interestingly, murderers were allowed bail not witches…). Worried as they were that Helen could somehow divulge information about D-Day, the Admiralty were determined to keep her in prison.

The reaction of the public was immediate: Helen's supporters organised a fund to pay for expenses of the defence witnesses and the Spiritualists National Union appointed Charles Loseby, a well-known barrister, to defend her against the charge. As the trial got underway, it caused a sensation in the newspapers. At one stage, the defence announced that Mrs. Duncan was prepared to demonstrate her abilities in the witness box. This amounted to conducting a séance in the court while in a state of trance. After considering the proposal throughout the night, the prosecution refused the offer.

The witnesses' testimony at Helen Duncan's trial is in itself a gold mine of evidence in support of the hypothesis of survival, and it has in fact been analyzed in some depth by experts in recent years (Manfred Cassirer, 1996). Forty-four witnesses appeared in court testifying to Helen's credibility, and three hundred more were ready to take the stand. From Cassirer's review we learn from instance that:

- Air Force Wing Commander George Mackie stated on oath that through Helen Duncan's materialization gifts he actually met his 'dead' mother and father and a brother.

- James Duncan (no relation), a jeweller, testified that both he and his daughter had seen his wife materialize on eight different occasions, in good light. Duncan had seen her close up at a range of 18 inches and they had talked of domestic matters including a proposed emigration to Canada that they had previously kept secret. He had, he said, not a shadow of a doubt that the voice was that of his wife. He also claimed to have seen materializations of his father, who was about his own height and bearded, and his mother.

- Mary Blackwell, President of the Pathfinder Spiritualist Society of Baker Street London, testified that she had attended more than 100 materialization séances with Helen Duncan at each of which between 15 and 16 different entities from the afterlife had materialized. She testified that she had witnessed the spirit forms conversing with their relatives in French, German, Dutch, Welsh, Scottish and Arabic. She claimed that she had witnessed the manifestation of ten of her own close relatives including her husband, her mother and her father all of whom she had seen up close and touched.

Despite no evidence having been found during the police raid and despite the defence witnesses' testimony, the jury found Helen Duncan guilty under the terms of the old Witchcraft Act. She was found innocent of all the other charges. The defence's right to appeal to the House of Lords was withheld. After being sentenced to nine months imprisonment, all she had to say was "I never hee'd so mony lies in a' my life".

What happened afterwards?

The end of this story is sad. It's one of the very human, very "real life" endings that I like in movies or books. Helen was released from prison in Sptember 1944 and, as she left prison, she vowed not to do psychic work ever again. She was not able, however, to resist the strong call from the Spirit world, and after a few months she resumed her work.

Things were not looking up, though. The experience of the trial and the time she had spent in prison had affected her badly. She would spend more and more time in trance. Perhaps too much so, for the quality of her séances deteriorated even to the point where Spiritualism's governing National Union actually withdrew her diploma at one stage. Meanwhile, Helen's diabetes and heart condition deteriorated: once a huge woman, she lost over 50 kilos of weight towards the end of her life.

Such an end was to come dramatically in late 1956. On Sunday, 26 October, for reasons that remain unknown to this day, the police raided again one of Helen's séances in the midlands city of Nottingham. They grabbed her, pinned her to the floor, strip searched her and took endless flashlight photographs, shouting that they were looking for beards, masks and shrouds. Again, they found nothing.

What they did, instead, was to commit the worst possible sin in psychical phenomena: to touch a trance medium during materialization. As the Spirit teachers have patiently explained so many times, when this happens the ectoplasm recoils into the medium's body far too quickly and can cause serious - sometimes even fatal - damage.

And so it was in this case: Helen was taken home with great difficulty and four days later Gena, one of her daughters and a trained nurse, discovered an angry burn the size of a tea plate on her right breast and a smaller one on her stomach, both apparently caused by the recoil of the ectoplasm. A doctor was summoned and described the burns as electrical, and doubted that they could be self-inflicted. She was so ill that she was rushed to hospital.

Five weeks after the police raid, Helen Duncan, mother of six and one of the brightest stars in the mediums' firmament, was dead.

Day 10 - Direct Voice mediumship

I think I can safely say I am the most tested medium this country has ever produced... I have been boxed up, tied up, sealed up, gagged, bound and held, and still the voices have come to speak their message of life eternal.

Leslie Flint

Do you remember what Gordon Smith, the Glasgow-based medium, does?

Yes – he channels communications from the spirit world.

Fine, but how does he do it?

He tells people what the communicators in the spirit world tell him.

Very good! That is what we defined as mental mediumship. As we have seen, good mental mediums are rare. I'd like to quote Professor Archie Roy when he said "There is, of course, a wide spectrum of mediumistic ability, from marvelous to mediocre. It would appear that as with almost any other human activity there are superstars, stars and barely luminous glow-worms!"

Why are you saying this now?

Because direct voice mediumship is even rarer than good mental mediumship.

And what does a direct voice medium do?

He or she does nothing in fact. The medium, with his/her presence, makes it possible for communicators from the spirit world to speak directly to the sitters.

You mean through the voice of the medium?

No, I mean through independent voices sometimes coming out of "trumpets" (metal cones used to somehow amplify these sounds), sometimes produced by ectoplasm and sometimes just coming out of thin air.

You certainly are not serious...

I am extremely serious. In fact, direct voice is a subset of what we call "physical mediumship", that is mediumship accompanied by physical phenomena. Such phenomena consist indeed of the creation of voices and other sounds, but also rapping, movement of objects (including the trumpets, which often fly around the room tapping lightly the person the next communication is addressed to), other forms of touch, and, most strikingly, what we'll describe in detail in a few days – spirit lights.

Aw, come on, come on now!

I know. I know it all seems completely absurd. The best thing we can do, then, is to look at how things work in practice. To do so, we'll focus on the phenomenal physical mediumship of Leslie Flint, the medium who provided the quote I used at the beginning.

The beginning of Leslie Flint's story is practically identical to what many other gifted mediums have told us - his faculties were already apparent during his early childhood, and the fact that he could see and somehow interact with deceased people caused him significant trouble with family and friends during the years of his youth. Funnily enough, in his 1971 autobiography Flint recounts that the first manifestations of paranormal voices consisted of persistent whispers around him as he was sitting in the darkness of a cinema, to the great annoyance of his fellow cinema-goers.

When he started formal sittings, people attending the séances were astonished to hear voices materializing independently from the medium's own vocal activity, and especially to recognize those voices as the ones of deceased friends and relatives.

90

Leslie Flint is particularly interesting for us, first because his rapid rise to popularity attracted the attention of numerous serious researchers and secondly because he lived in a time when electronic recording was widely available. Thousands of the voices recorded during his séances are still available today - just make a search on the Internet and you'll find plenty. Listening to those recordings is in itself a highly educational - if a bit eerie - experience.

What about fraud? Such voices must be easy to produce in a dark room where people can't see what you're doing.

Oh yes? Like, how?

Well, you just change the tone of your voice, put on an accent - something like that...

With your mouth sealed with horizontal and vertical strips of surgical tape, the position of which is marked on the skin with indelible pencil, and your hands tied to the chair?

Oh...

Or in broad electric light?

Uh-oh...

Or rather with a hand of a researcher permanently on your mouth, or a microphone taped to your larynx or a quantity of coloured water that you have to keep in your mouth and has to be the same before and after the séance?

Have all these experiments actually been carried out?

All of them, by independent researchers including Drayton Thomas, Professor of Psychiatry at the University of Cambridge.

And with all these controls in place voices could still be heard?

As loud and clear as during uncontrolled séances.

Gosh - this is really hard to swallow. Could he not be a ventriloquist?

I am sorry, but ventriloquists are not "ventriloquists", that is – they don't "speak from their tummies"! What a ventriloquist does is talk through the mouth, with minimal movements of the lips and whilst focusing the attention of the listeners onto the dummy.

No ventriloquism, then. What about accomplices? Associates who would sneak into the room and...

...and never be detected, not once, in thousands of séances? No, look, that is untenable. And, what makes the "conspiracy" theory almost laughable are some pretty common sense considerations. To explore that, I need to introduce another very gifted but perhaps less known physical medium, John Sloan, and the researcher who thoroughly investigated him, Arthur Findlay.

John Sloan was another Glasgow native, a packer in a warehouse, and a small shopkeeper. His relative lack of notoriety is probably due to his persistent refusal to become a public medium, to take money for his work, or to give demonstrations. Sloan himself had little interest for mediumship, and conducted sittings solely for the benefit of others. Arthur Findlay describes him as "an upright, good, honest man, with little learning, poor memory, and ...average intelligence".

To have the medium at the disposal of the British College of Psychic Science, at some stage Hewat McKenzie found employment for Sloan in a London garage and made him accessible to various experimenters. After his return to Glasgow, he was experimented with for five years by Arthur Findlay, a successful stockbroker, a Justice of the Peace and the founder of the Glasgow Society for Psychical Research. In 1924 he published a small book on his findings: *An Investigation of Psychic Phenomena* with a preface by Sir William Barrett. This was followed by a larger volume: *On the Edge of the Etheric*, in 1931.

What makes Findlay's investigation of John Sloan particularly interesting is that he provides verbatim accounts of 24 séances held between April 1942 and July 1945, taken down by an expert stenographer, Miss Jean Darie. The séances in question, attended by between seven and eleven sitters each, were all held in Glasgow at the homes of various of the sitters, and never in Sloan's own home. Findlay went as far as sending copies of the verbatim transcripts to seven of the regular sitters and obtained signed statements that the accounts agreed with their own notes taken at the time.

Now, back to the issue of accomplices and fraud. First, let's consider that Sloan held regular séances for over 50 years, usually in other people's homes and in front of many reliable witnesses, without any charge of trickery ever being made against him. Secondly, let' see what Findlay had to say on what would have been necessary if trickery were to take place.

1. Sloan would have had to engage a script writer to help him think up a new script for each sitting that reflected the many sitters who, at different times, regularly attended his séances over some 50 years, and a knowledge of such details of any dead friends and relatives who might communicate. Such knowledge would have had to include pet names used within families, together with other details of intricate family relationships.

2. The scripts would also have had to include appropriate material for many hundreds of other sitters who came as guests of the regular circle members, many of whom protected their anonymity before and during the sitting and yet still received satisfactory communications.

3. Accomplices would have been needed for each sitting in order to impersonate, from different positions in the room, the 40 or so characters who appeared in the script for each sitting and spoke through the independent voice method.

4. The accomplices would have had to be smuggled into the various private houses where the sittings were held, bringing with them any necessary props. In addition to using their voices, they would have had to keep two trumpets flying around the room, frequently at a great speed, and even touching the ceiling and beating on it, ring bells, and make small lights dance so expertly here and there that they were never caught by the sitters.

5. The accomplices would have had to manage all this in the dark, and in small rooms where most of the space was taken up by sitters, and without bumping into the sitters or into each other.

6. In addition, the accomplices would have had to find sitters unerringly in the dark in order to touch them – often on request – and to stroke and caress their faces.

7. Finally, the accomplices would have had to escape undetected from the room before the electric lights were switched on at the end of the sitting.

I'm speechless. So much evidence, so much investigation and reflection, so much depth...

I know. I know exactly how you feel. Let me, if you will, take advantage of this moment of realization and go a bit more in depth. I would really like to try to "drive the concept home", so to speak. To do that, I need your undivided attention for another wee while.

Go ahead, I'm all ears.

Very good. Let me start with one of my questions. Would you be able to cross a ditch by walking on a single bamboo stick?

Of course not.

And if you tied two or three together ?

Same thing – they would break under my weight.

And if you tied 20 or 30 together?

Then, probably I could.

And, finally, what about a couple of hundred?

With that, I could probably cross with a small car!

Even if a few sticks were relatively weak?

Definitely. It's the collective strength of the sticks that counts.

Good. This, I believe, provides a very good image of why I personally consider the evidence for survival conclusive. Follow my thinking: so far we have considered a large number of pieces of evidence, and we'll look at many more in the next days. I believe that you yourself were struck by how convincing many of these were, even if taken alone.

Yes – I must admit you're right.

Fine. However, here I am not maintaining that each individual piece of evidence is proven beyond any doubt. Mind you - I am personally convinced of that in many cases, but that is not the point right now. I am perfectly ready to admit that not all evidence is proven beyond doubt, and

I am not even interested in debating any further if this or that particular piece of evidence is proven or not. What I am maintaining is that the *collective* weight of the evidence, based on thousands upon thousands of individual pieces, proves beyond any reasonable doubt that elements of the human personality somehow survive physical death and are capable of interacting with those who are still in this life.

We have seen what extremes skeptics have gone to in order to disprove some pieces of evidence, and failed. We have just seen that the survival hypothesis is at times less incredible than alternative, more "rational" explanations. Now think for a moment of the stories I've told you, and of the ones I haven't told you yet (you remember – less than ten percent of what I myself read, which is less that one percent of what's available in literature....). See these as bamboo sticks, tied together with one very solid string: the fact that, no matter how diverse, they are all consistent with the survival hypothesis – almost to the point of making any other explanation outlandish. Think about what conclusions you draw yourself from this collective evidence.

Before we end today's conversation, I would like to tell you one particular story about Sloan and Findlay that I found not only very touching, but also shows the lengths to which psychic researchers will go in order to test the validity of the information they gather from mediums in the course of their investigations. This episode happened in 1919 and the central character is John, Arthur Findlay's brother.

One day, Arthur took John - who had been demobilized from the army a few weeks earlier - to one of Sloan's séances. Obviously, Arthur did not introduce his brother either to the medium, nor to any of the sitters attending that particular day. Needless to say, there was no way for anybody to know that John had been a soldier, or that he had spent part of his military service training machine gunners at Lowestoft on the East Coast of England, and at Kessingland, a small village nearby.

At a certain moment during the sitting, John Findlay was startled to feel the trumpet tap lightly on his knee and to hear a voice announce itself as "Eric Saunders". John confessed that he could not think of anybody he knew by that name, and asked Eric Saunders where they might have met. The following conversation was then recorded:

Saunders: In the army.

Findlay: Aldershot? Bisley? France? Palestine?

Saunders: No, none of these places. I knew you when you were near Lowestoft.

Findlay: Near Lowestoft?

Saunders: You were not in Lowestoft then, but at Kessingland.

Findlay: To which company were you attached?

Saunders: *B? C?* (answer not clear)

Findlay: Can you remember the name of your Company Commander?

Saunders: *MacNamara* (correct for Company Commander of the B Company)

Findlay: (testing Saunders by pretending to remember him) *Oh, yes, you were one of my Lewis gunners were you not?*

Saunders: *No, you had not the Lewis guns then, it was the Hotchkiss* (the Hotchkiss machine gun replaced the Lewis guns in 1917)

The exchange then went on as Findlay asked a few more leading questions, which Saunders answered correctly. Then, it was Saunders who said:

Saunders: We had great times there, Sir, do you remember the General's inspection?

Findlay: To which inspection do you refer?

Saunders: *The day the General made us race about with the guns.* (Findlay remembered this incident well, and the fact that it had caused a great deal of amusement among the troops).

Then Saunders provided details of his own death, which had happened in France.

Findlay: When did you go to France?

Saunders: With the big draft of August 1917.

Findlay: Why do you call it the big draft?

Saunders: *Don't you remember the big draft, when the Colonel came on the parade ground and made a speech?* (Findlay remembered that a particularly large draft had indeed gone out to France in August 1917. That was the only occasion he could remember when the Colonel ever personally said good-bye to the men.)

Understandably, this episode made a big impression on John Findlay, to the point that he decided to try to verify the information that had been provided to him. It took him six months to trace the corporal who had been his assistant with the light guns at Kessingland. When a meeting was finally arranged, the corporal consulted a pocket diary in which he had kept a full list of the men under training with Findlay. He looked up the records for B Company in 1917: sure enough "Eric Saunders, fully qualified August 1917" appeared in his notes. The corporal's notes also indicated that Eric Saunders had gone out to France with the draft that same August.

Day 11 - Materialization mediumship

I shall not waste time in stating the absurdities, almost the impossibilities, from a psycho-physiological point of view, of this phenomenon. A living being, or living matter, formed under our eyes, which has its proper warmth, apparently a circulation of blood, and a physiological respiration which has also a kind of psychic personality having a will distinct from the will of the medium, in a word, a new human being! This is surely the climax of marvels. Nevertheless, it is a fact.
Prof. Charles Richet – Nobel Prize winner for Medicine, 1913

This, as I hinted a couple of days ago, is the most difficult of our conversations for me to have.

Mmm... I don't remember you saying that. Why do you say difficult?

Well, for three reasons. The first is that, as Prof. Richet says in the quote, we will be talking absurdities. I know that we have already touched upon some utterly unbelievable pieces of evidence, but with the extremes of physical mediumship I feel that my own acceptance capacity is stretched almost beyond limits. Somehow, I find it less difficult to accept that the blind can see during NDEs, or that communicators from the Spirit world provide pieces of information that nobody – not the medium, not the sitters – possessed and that turns out to be astoundingly accurate. But to have lights dancing around the séance room, heavy pieces of furniture and/or the mediums levitate, physical objects appearing out of thin air and remaining stably in this world and , well, *body parts and even entire persons materializing out of nothing and interacting with the investigators* is in a way too much.

The second reason is that the more readily available and widely used explanation – fraud – turned out to be true in a number of cases.

Aha! Now you talk some sense!

I know, it's somehow comforting, isn't it? Things falling back into our beloved "logical" and "sensible" understanding of reality, based on our everyday experience. The problem, particularly for me, in light of my own difficulties, is that it appears that for each and every case in which fraud was proven, there are many others in which no evidence of fraud whatsoever was ever discovered, and a certain number of cases in which the calibre of the people involved in the investigations and the controls put in place make the case for fraud or trickery simply untenable.

Let's talk fraud, then.

Hold on a minute, if you will. I first need to tell you about my third difficulty, which is also big but more subtle, and about the reflections I've made after researching the subject in literature.

Ok, go ahead.

First of all, you have to know that physical mediumship is a lot rarer now than it used to be. Some say that this is due to better investigation methods, and therefore that this is further proof that physical phenomena are nothing more than conjuror's tricks. This, as we'll see in due course, is a very shallow argument, as strict and – relatively speaking – technologically advanced protocols were used already in the 1870's. Others point to emergence of different forms of physical mediumship such as the energy-based phenomena recently produced during the Scole experiment. Be it as it may, it is true that, although some notable physical mediums are active today, most of the evidence cmes from the past.

It so happens that, as I began studying the subject, I was immediately drawn to the ample photographic evidence available from the early decades of last century. I remember distinctly looking at some of the yellowish pictures hanging in the library of the Glasgow Association of Spiritualists, and feeling bad.

Feeling bad?

Yes, feeling somehow robbed, deprived – like something had been taken away from me. At that time, I was already in some depth into the subject of survival, and, following the "many sticks" approach, I had come to the conclusions we've talked about yesterday. Some of the pictures I was looking at seemed to tell me that all that, after all, was false and that I, like so many others, just *wanted to believe*.

Sorry, I don't understand.

Oh, well, just look at this, please.

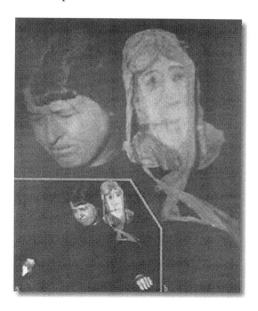

What is it?

It's a picture of a materialization of a medium known as Eva C, thoroughly investigated by Baron von Schrenck-Notzing, a German physician, during the 1910's and 1920's. What does it look like?

A joke.

Does it not? A childish, crude attempt to reproduce something vaguely resembling a ghost.

Yes I agree. And I do understand how you feel – if this is what materialization is all about, we may as well stop our conversation here.
Well, no. Materialization, even in the past, is actually a lot more than this. But for the moment let's stay with this picture – and with the similar ones like those I saw in Glasgow.

What else about the Eva C picture?

You know, I stayed with this pocket of frustration for a while, and then decided to take some time and research this a bit further. What I found was actually quite puzzling: the picture we've looked at was taken under extremely strict conditions, and the more I thought about it the more I was drawn to... No, hold on a sec. Let me explain properly.

First of all, let's see how Baron von Schrenck-Notzing himself describes the materialization during the particular séance in which the picture was taken:

"Between 9 p.m. and 9.10 p.m. without the help of the hands or knees, a flowing white substance emerged from the medium's mouth, which was inclined towards the left. It was about 20 inches long and 8 inches broad. It lay on the breast of the dress, spread out, and formed a white head-like disk, with a face profile turned to the right, and of life size. Even after the flash-light was ignited the curtain remained wide open. At the same moment the author illuminated the structure with an electric torch, and found that it formed a folded strip, which receded slowly into the medium's mouth, and remained visible until the sitting closed at 9.20 p.m."

Now, in terms of the controls, let's see what Montague Keen has to say in *A Study in Critical Analysis of Paranormal Physical Phenomena*:

"Among the most frequently reproduced photographs designed to illustrate the obviously fraudulent nature of so-called ectoplasmic images of the past are those of somewhat grotesque and crude paper masks. They featured in Baron von Schrenck Notzing's celebrated series of tests on a medium known to history as Eva C. But a study of the elaborate precautions taken by the medical investigator and his two qualified colleagues shows that, if Eva had contrived to smuggle in the mask during the séance of August 7th 1912, she would have had to have packed and concealed about her body a plastic mask of natural size, a head shape of paper or textile fabric, and a quantity of a substance, the size of a hand, which would leave traces on her dress.

In spite of all the precautions, including prior examination of her bare body, hair, mouth and ears, and being sewn into a séance costume which was found after the sitting to have remained unopened, the medium would have had to pack this equipment in or on her body, open it up, use it before the cameras, fold it all up again and conceal around her bare body so that it would remain undetected despite a subsequent body search. Precautions extended to hand-holding and the unexpected shining of torches and taking of flashlight plates."

Finally, let's also consider that Baron von Schrenck-Notzing was well aware of the critics' claims that Eva C produced her materializations by regurgitating "chiffon gauze, rubber gloves, such as are used for operations, objects cut out in the shape of hands, formless shreds of animal mesentery, as well as catgut, and the like, which can be inflated" which she would have swallowed before the séance. Here is what he writes concerning the end of the séance:

"While in the state of hypnosis, the medium rose from her chair and took an emetic tendered to her by the author (1 gram ipecacuanha and 1/2 gram tartar emetic), was completely undressed while standing half in and half out of the cabinet, and examined in detail by the author and Dr Bourbon, who took charge of the séance costume, and also examined it carefully. The final examination of the cabinet and chair gave no result. Dressed in a dressing-gown, Eva C. was then laid on a couch in the room, and was not left unobserved for a moment.

After two further doses of the same strength, vomiting set in at 9.30 p.m., which brought up the contents of the stomach. The quantity was about a pint, and was taken charge of by the author, who did not give it out of his hands until he handed it over to the Masselin Laboratory in Paris for analysis. The vomit was brown in colour, and besides the wafers taken with the powders there was no trace of any white substance such as observed by us. The detailed report of the Laboratory in question, closes with the words:

The final result of the examination shows that the vomit consisted exclusively of food products and the emetics, and contained fragments of meat, fruit, and vegetables, probably mushrooms, which were found in pieces of considerable size. The rest of the contents consisted of food in an advanced state of digestion. There was not the slightest trace of a body whose appearance or histological structure gave the impression of a foreign body, or of a substance not used for nutrition, and, in particular, there was no trace of paper or chiffon."

Now were does this leave us?

It leaves us – or at least me – completely frazzled.

Please explain.

Well, it's like… reason being stuck between a rock and a hard place.

As in?

As in being stuck between equally unlikely alternatives.

Lay them out for me, will you?

Well, first the Baron could have invented everything. He could have placed the picture himself and then taken the photograph. Or he could have enlisted the other two doctors in his deception scheme – that is, no examination of the medium took place before or after the séance, no sewn costume, no controls. The vomit was collected from somebody else, or the laboratory report was faked.

Fine. That's a possibility. Just consider what an aristocrat and respected physician of the early 1900's would stand to gain from such a complicated deception, and answer yourself as to the likelihood of that possibility. What other alternative do you see?

That things went as the Baron described. That this somewhat pitiful image was created paranormally.

And?

And… I don't know. I somehow wonder - why the Spirit world should bother creating something so simple, so ordinary…

Right. But then, here we come to the considerations that I – and many scholars much better informed than me – have made in respect to this. Who are we to expect anything? We don't know a thing about the intentions and capacities of those on the other side, we completely ignore the mechanisms by which materializations take place, and still, to fit our preconceived ideas, we expect something dramatic, something so clearly "otherworldly" as to satisfy our desire for the exceptional. Instead of marveling at the fact that something – no matter what – flows out of the mouth of a medium and takes whatever shape, is photographed, and then flows back and completely disappears, we feel disappointed. Many paranormal phenomena are no less simple and ordinary – raps, noises, lights – and still we find *that* fascinating and intriguing.

Er… I think I see what you are saying. I need some time to think it over.

Ok. Whilst you think, you may have a look at something considerably more exotic…

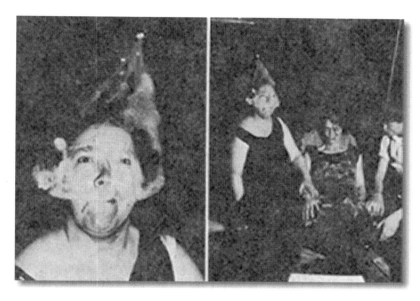

... check out the impressive snapshot (following page) taken during a session in full darkness (you can make out the reflection of the flashlight on the ceiling, the luminous bands attached to the extremities of the chair to check its movements in darkness, the medium, gagged, sitting against the far wall, and the expression and movement of the sitters, caught in their shock at the wild movements of the chair)...

...and learn about Katie King, the spirit control of medium Florence Cook, who provided some of the most spectacular and widely investigated materializations in history. Let's see what Dr. J. M. Gully, a physician and a careful investigator, has to say:

"That the power grows with use was curiously illustrated by the fact that, for some time, only a face was producible, with, occasionally, arms and hands; with no hair, and sometimes with no back to the skull at all - merely a mask, with movement, however, of eyes and mouth. Gradually the whole form appeared - after, perhaps, some five months of séances once or twice a week. This again became more and more rapidly formed, and changed, in hair, dress, and color of face, as we desired.

The voice came long before the whole form of the body, but was always husky, and as if there was a whispering catarrh; save when she joined us in singing, when she gave out a most lovely contralto.

The feel of the skin was quite natural, soft and warm; her movements were natural and graceful, except when she stooped to pick up anything from the floor, when it seemed as if her legs as well as her trunk bent backwards."

And now, turn the page a have a look at Katie King herself, in a beautiful, dramatic close-up.

Day 12 - Physical mediumship today

You may remember I told you that physical mediumship seems to be a lot rarer today than it used to be during the first few decades of last century.

Yes I do, and I also remember that you told me that many say this is because of the increased controls.

Indeed you are right – many skeptics say so. However, you will agree with me that it is quite difficult to think of anything more stringent than the controls applied during the sessions with Eva C.

Agreed.

And that was 1907... Plus, let me tell you that, from what I read, those controls were pretty much the standard procedure utilized when investigating mediums. I think that it is very wrong to assume that investigators of the past would be less careful, more naive, more easily deceived than anybody today.

But you have to admit that people one century ago knew less than we know today, and there was inevitably more room, psychologically speaking, for the unknown, the inexplicable.

Yes, I agree. That's the reason why today I would like to do a little "role play" simulation exercise with you. I'll ask you to play the role of a modern day researcher who sets out to investigate the claims of a physical medium. I'll ask you to set the experimental conditions, to think of the controls you would like to put in place in order to satisfy yourself that what you are witnessing cannot be the result of fraud, trickery or simple deception.

Very good – that sounds interesting.

Then, step by step, we will compare your requirements with the procedures employed during two separate but very similar experiments (2003 and 2006) investigating Australian physical medium David Thompson. To do so, I will refer to the very detailed reports produced respectively by Montague Keen, a member of the Council of the Society for Psychical Research for 55 years, and Victor Zammit, an Australian lawyer, author of a well-known publication and a knowledgeable and articulate advocate for the theme of survival.

OK – I'm ready to go.

Good. I have to make things more difficult for you, though.

In what sense?

In the sense that the séances you will investigate have to take place in complete darkness. At some stage, you will be allowed to switch on a red light to witness materializations, but otherwise it's got to be darkness.

But that's an open invitation for fraud!

That is exactly why things are more complicated for you. You have to satisfy yourself that no tricks took place even if you could not see the medium very well.

And what's the reason for this requirement?

Hold on – who is producing the physical phenomena?

The medium.

Wrong – it's Spirit. It's the disincarnate personalities who have apparently survived physical death who are responsible for anything happening. The medium is simply there to provide a channel for Spirit to communicate and to make things happen.

And...

And, communicators from the Spirit world have been telling us for over 150 years and with varying degrees of detail (including in-depth technical discussions with scientists) that electric light and even infrared light make it very difficult for them to come through and make things happen. There have been several occasions in which extraordinary phenomena where produced in broad daylight, but these are exceptions. More often, things have been recorded on video tape through infra-red sensors, but in your case, unless you are told to switch on the red light, you will have to stick with near-complete darkness.

Well, OK then. I'll keep this in mind.

Thanks. And now, let's start. In thinking of your controls, please take into consideration that you are expecting to witness direct voices and macroscopic physical phenomena, such as the movement of objects, sounds, touches. I would like you to take your time, perhaps jot down a well-thought list of controls before you start.

Are you ready ?

Yes, I'm ready.

Fire off, then.

Well, the first thing I would like to have control over is the physical environment. I don't want to hold the séance in the medium's house or in a place the medium knows well or can control.

Very good. Our 2006 reference experiment took place in a private house near Sidney, Australia, previously unknown to the medium. The 2003 experiment took place halfway around the world, in Oxfordshire, UK.

Fine. Then, still in terms of physical environment, I would like to be absolutely sure that the room where the séance takes place has no hidden recesses, hidden doors, disguised equipment and does not contain anything that can be used to play tricks in the dark.

All right. Have a look at what Keen had to say in 2003…

"There was only one door into the séance room, which had no windows, was perfectly rectangular except for a recess at one end of the room (120 cm x 60 cm x 210 cm high) which formed the back half of the cabinet, and was devoid of ornaments or recesses. The room measured roughly 4.5 m x 3 m, and at one end carried a rectangular ceiling rail from which three floor-length black curtains were suspended by Velcro straps of curtaining material, so that the curtains could be opened and closed from both sides. This, along with the recess, constituted the cabinet. The room was seamlessly carpeted throughout. Apart from the entrance door from the anteroom, there were no detectable orifices beyond five small vents in the ceiling and three low-level vents along one wall, vented to the outside. Moulded plastic seats were placed around all the walls save the cabinet end. Two of the seats blocked the entrance door, and that occupied by my wife obstructed the door from being opened."

…and Zammit in 2006:

"The room was a small lounge-dining room in a middle class suburban rented house in a quiet area. At the end of the room where we were sitting the windows had been blocked out and there was no furniture except for a number of straight backed chairs and a large modular display cabinet about 2.5 meters tall in which it would have been impossible to conceal even a small person. There were no trapdoors –walls, floors and ceiling or recesses in the room. Once everyone was seated, the only door to the room was locked and the key given to me. A large sheet of cardboard was stuck over the door to block any light and to seal the only door to the séance room. A chair was placed behind the door underneath the doorknob for added security."

OK, that sounds good. Now, I would turn my attention to the sitters. They should introduce no objects or equipment that could be used to produce the phenomena.

Good thinking. See how our investigators addressed those concerns:

Keen: "The room (…) was entered via an anteroom where all those attending were asked to leave behind loose jewellery, handbags, watches, pens, wallets, money: indeed anything which could be detached."

Zammit: "All of the other sitters were searched and asked to leave outside anything metal, lighters, matches, mobile phones etc."

And the medium?

There we go:

Keen: "I searched David Thompson and ascertained there was nothing in any trousers pocket or concealed on his singlet, over which he wore a cardigan which I searched separately before he replaced it. I also checked his trainer-type shoes to ascertain that the heels and soles were normal and unified."

Zammit: "Prior to entering the room I was asked to search the medium and confirm that he had nothing under his clothing. Another sitter and I checked his track pants, pockets, his cardigan and his shoes to make sure that they were normal."

So far so good. Now, probably the most important precaution would be to make sure that the medium could not move, and that he could not in any way produce sounds with his mouth.

Right. Follow these descriptions carefully, and see if investigators indeed addressed your concerns.

Keen: "The chair in which the medium sat was an old-fashioned upholstered, heavy, wooden construction which I examined carefully, having regard to a claim by the magician Ian Rowland, when commenting on television on Thompson's reputed feats, that this could be done by illusionists when the ends of the chair arms were not securely connected to the posts, thereby enabling the medium to raise his arms from the post and slip the cable ties off his arms. I could find no loose connections, and was unable to move the arms or see or feel anything abnormal underneath the chair.

The chair was placed inside the open cabinet, and the medium was strapped into it by means of plastic tree ties. This was effected by Bianca (the medium's wife) under my close supervision. I was invited to examine the ties which were already permanently fixed to the legs and arms of the chair, both before and after the fixing. The straps were placed through these permanent fixings, and pulled tight, and then secured with thin plastic ties with the ends trimmed off, so that the only way to release the bond was to cut it. The straps were so tightly pulled that I was unable to intrude even a finger. Indeed, the medium subsequently was heard to complain that his wife had been so enthusiastic as to cause him discomfort. Bianca tied a black gag securely round the medium's head through his open mouth, thereby preventing recognisable speech. I examined the gag and the knot behind the head."

Zammit: "The chair on which the medium sat was a metal one. The arms were securely fastened, there were no loose connections and there was nothing unusual beneath the chair. The chair was placed in the corner of the room. The sitters sat in a semi-circle facing the medium. The medium was strapped into the chair by means of secure belts and buckles firmly attached to the chair.

As well, heavy plastic one-way (self-locking) cable ties were secured through the buckles and cut off short so that the only way they could be released was with a metal clipper. I checked that the bindings were reasonably tight and that the medium could not slip either arm back out of the ties.
The medium had a black gag tied securely around his head through his open mouth preventing him from making any more than muffled sounds. I checked the knot and helped secure a cable tie to the gag."

Now, before we go on, please note that a very weird phenomenon had been known to occur involving David Thompson's cardigan. The investigators therefore noted:

Keen: "Finally the several buttons on the front of medium's cardigan were tied into the buttonholes with thin black strips of plastic. These are one-way (self-locking) cable ties, incapable of being untied. They have to be cut before a button can be released."

Zammit: "As well cable ties were used to tie the buttons of the medium's cardigan to the buttonholes and clipped off very short."

OK, I don't understand, but I've noted that.

Good. Anything else?

Again, I would like to be sure that nothing special is in the room.

There we go:

Keen: "On the floor a few feet in front of the medium there was a black coated piece of board, about 180 cm by 60. After I had checked underneath to satisfy myself that nothing was concealed below it, the following items were placed on it: a cardboard trumpet, the end of which was coated with luminous paint; a mouth organ; a rattle, and two drum sticks, all of which were to play a part in the séance. In addition there was a pair of pliers which were employed by Bianca to cut the ties to release her husband after the sitting, and two wooden rings which were brought into the room from the anteroom at the medium's request after my wife had taken a number of photographs.
A microphone was suspended from the wall near the door, the other end being connected to a Sony personal tape recorder located on a small table. The only other equipment was a small flexible table lamp with a red bulb and fixed shade. It was placed on a small table in the corner on the medium's left, outside the curtain, together with a glass of water. In the opposite corner was a large tape recorder playing music. The light was controlled by Paul who sat alongside me, while the music player was the responsibility of Bianca, who had to make frequent changes in the music played and the volume requested, at the behest of spirit communicators. Both Paul's hands held my right hand throughout the séance, save for about five minutes when they were needed to switch on and manoeuvre the light during the brief period when ectoplasmic extrusions were being shown."

Zammit : "On the mantelpiece in the room was a set of drum sticks and a glass of water. Beside the séance leader's chair was a CD player with a music CD, a small lamp with red globes and a simple cardboard cone, the end of which was lined with luminous tape. In physical mediumship circles this is called a *trumpet* and is used as a simple megaphone to amplify spirit voices.

Thirty minutes prior to the beginning of the séance we set in motion an MP3 recorder with a very sensitive microphone which recorded the entire 90 minute session."

Well, not being in a laboratory, I think that this is more or less as far as I would go in terms of precautions. What happened during the séances, then?

Unless we want to spend hours on this, we have to stick to the summaries provided by the two authors. Let's see how Montague Keen recaps the phenomena:

"The evening was notable for the clarity and fluency of the two principal communicators, who introduced themselves as William Charles Cadwell, (died 1897) and Sir William Crookes both of whom invited and answered questions. Two other voices familiar to the regular participants also came through: a cockney youth named Timothy Booth, and Louis Armstrong. Both had very distinctive features and claimed to have materialised. Timothy was responsible for the widespread reports of touches and boisterous noises, as well as the delicate management of the ectoplasm and the ordering of the correct degree of red light to enable us to see the medium but not harm him.

In terms of physical phenomena, the following were reported.

1. The trumpet, the luminous large end of which was seen to be performing a variety of patterns and aerobic adornments in the air, was operated at great speed and with considerable precision, and was pressed quite hard against my chest at one stage.

2. My head was tapped sharply several times, apparently by the luminous end of the trumpet during the aerial demonstrations.

3. I was vigorously slapped on both knees as an introduction to the first supposedly materialised entity.

4. My tie was unknotted, ripped off, and thrust with great precision in the narrow space between the chairs on which my wife and I were sitting. It was later found on the carpet beneath the chairs.

5. The appearance some time during the séance of a cut on the lower

side of the base of my right thumb. It was made without my knowledge or awareness, and was some 2cm in length with congealed blood along the line of what would have normally been considered to be a scratch. My wife's pre-séance picture shows no sign of any cut on my hand, whereas that taken immediately after the sitting does. My hand was held firmly by my immediate neighbour, Paul, throughout the sitting, normally with both hands, save for the few minutes required for him to adjust the red light. The scar was still faintly visible twelve days later.

6. The two rings of equal dimensions but different woods were found on the left arm of Alan, sitting opposite me and alongside Bianca. Towards the end of the séance he had reported that someone was trying to force the rings over his wrist. When I tried to pull them over his hand to remove them he complained that it was painful, although later succeeded in doing so. He contrasted this with the relatively gentle pressure experienced when the rings had been pushed over his wrist during the séance.

7. While holding my wife's right hand with my left, leaving my index finger protruding, we were both touched by a warm, soft and seemingly human hand for about fifteen seconds.

8. There was tap dancing of an apparently expert kind, as well as extremely fast drumming on the ceiling during the Irish jig music.

9. A silver tie pin surmounted by a cat was apported as a gift to Bianca, purportedly through the mouth of the medium as he extruded ectoplasm.

10. At the end of the sitting, following the withdrawal of the final communicator, the light was slowly turned up. It revealed David Thompson still tied to his chair, and gagged, in the middle of the room, some two meters from its original position inside the cabinet. It had been moved over the top of the black board and its several instruments.

When the medium had recovered sufficiently to face the light, and the gag had been removed and retied to shield his eyes from the flashes, my wife took a number of post-sitting photographs. These included one showing the cardigan reversed. Having checked that the ties were still in place, I watched as Bianca used the pliers to cut each of the ties fixing the buttons to the buttonholes, and examined the arm and leg bindings as she cut the ties before the straps could be unfastened."

Hold on – you mean the cardigan was reversed with the medium tied to the chair *and the buttons tied with plastic bands?*

Pictures are there to show it. And this is what Victor Zammit reported in 2006:

"Before each entity materialized we heard and recorded a peculiar loud whooshing sound which can be heard in all of the MP3 recordings. There was a similar but shorter sound when entities dematerialized.

William, the control, welcomed everyone to the circle and introduced us to some spectacular movements of the trumpet. We could see the luminous end of it whizzing around the room. At times it passed just an inch (2 centimetres) away from our faces. We could feel a rush of air as it passed us. At one stage it repeatedly tapped myself and my partner on the head, moving rapidly from one of us to the other although we were separated by another person.

We heard seven definitively different voices which were clear, loud and distinctive with different pitch, rhythm, pace, intonation and modulation. All of the voices answered questions intelligently from the sitters, who could constantly hear each other asking questions from their original positions.

Often the entities would begin speaking using direct voice- an artificial larynx constructed from ectoplasm the sound coming from close to the medium. Then they would materialize with a distinctive sound and start to move around the room.

Several sitters commented on the abnormal cold around their feet and legs, something which is usually associated with the production of ectoplasm.

Several of the sitters were able to see the fingers of a materialized hand in the light of the luminous strips on the trumpet while it was held high in the air.

At the end of the meeting when the lights went on the medium was still bound and in his chair but the chair had been moved without a sound into the middle of the circle, about 2 meters from its original position and right in front of me. The medium's cardigan was still on, with the plastic ties still unbroken, but it had been reversed so that the buttons were up the medium's back."

And...

"Montague Keen - *the author of the 2003 report, who had passed away in 2004* - spoke directly to me by name and said he would be working with me to prove the existence of the afterlife."

Day 13 - Reincarnation studies

There are three claims in the [parapsychology] field which, in my opinion, deserve serious study," [the third being] "that young children sometimes report details of a previous life, which upon checking turn out to be accurate and which they could not have known about in any other way than reincarnation

Carl Sagan

Carl Sagan the astronomer?

Very much him.

Even I know him as a hardened skeptic!

True, but the quote shows that even the most close minded ones have at some point to surrender to the overwhelming evidence, just as our friend Ray Hyman had to do in the cases we've talked about in the early days.

And why are we talking reincarnation just now?

Because I felt that, after having talked physical mediumship for a couple of days – an area that even I still consider "borderline" – I had to take you back to full scientific respectability.

As in?

As in, to begin with, the studies carried out for nearly half a century by Prof. Ian Stevenson, who sadly passed away just a few months ago. Stevenson studied at St. Andrews University in Scotland and at McGill University in Montreal, where he received a B.S. in 1942 and an M.D. in 1943, graduating at the top of his class. In 1967, Stevenson was appointed as Director of the Division of Personality Studies (later renamed Division of Perceptual Studies) and, for a period was also Head of the Department of Psychiatry at the University of Virginia in the US.

Stevenson was indeed the founder of scientific research into reincarnation, and was best known for collecting and meticulously researching cases of children who seem to recall past lives without the need for hypnosis and for his extraordinary work on birthmarks in relation to apparent memories of previous lives.

The problem with Prof. Stevenson is that he published only for the academic and scientific community: his over 200 articles and several books - densely packed with research details and academic argument - are in places difficult for the average reader to follow. Just take as an example *Reincarnation and Biology: A Contribution to the Etiology of Birthmarks and Birth Defects*: this is a two-volume, 2268-page examination of cases in which persons were born with birthmarks or birth defects related to traumas purportedly suffered by a "previous personality," and medical records associated with such cases. I myself have read the 396 pages of *Twenty Cases Suggestive of Reincarnation*, published in 1974 by Virginia University Press, and I can assure you that it was no small feat!

You'll have to summarize it for me, then.

Yes – I'll try. But, for the sake of completeness, we have to go beyond the twenty cases discussed in the book I read. You have to remember that Prof. Stevenson carried out field research about reincarnation in Africa, Alaska, British Columbia, Burma, India, South America, Lebanon, Turkey, and many other places, and he reviewed over 3,000 individual cases. He describes his general approach as following an "almost conventional pattern":

> "The case usually starts when a small child of two to four years of age begins talking to his parents or siblings of a life he led in another time and place. The child usually feels a considerable pull back toward the events of the life and he frequently importunes his parents to let him return to the community where he claims that he formerly lived. If the child makes enough particular statements

about the previous life, the parents (usually reluctantly) begin inquiries about their accuracy. Often, indeed usually, such attempts at verification do not occur until several years after the child has begun to speak of the previous life. If some verification results, members of the two families visit each other and ask the child whether he recognizes places, objects, and people of his supposed previous existence."

In investigating such spontaneous life recall cases, Prof. Stevenson would carefully question both the family of the living child and the family of the deceased to ensure that they had no contact and that no information would be passed between them. He would obtain detailed information about the deceased, including information not fully known to anyone involved, such as details of the will, which he would use to verify that the child actually did know the information required. He would also personally and carefully vet each case to ensure that no other method of obtaining the information was possible for these children. This includes ensuring that the children were physically distant from the previous life described by them to rule out local knowledge being passed to the children. It also includes ensuring that their parents had never met nor had mutual friends who could have conveyed this information to the children. The interview process even includes taking possessions from the dead person and requiring the children pick out the objects amongst a field of random objects.

And the results?

The results are nothing short of stunning. I am tempted to report a few individual stories, to make you understand the absolutely incredible level of detail and consistency of the memories of the children, but I want to save time for later, when I'll tell you another quite extraordinary story which captures the issue of past memories quite well. The bottom line is that, after this enormous and painstaking work and after having thoroughly considered all possible alternatives, Prof. Stevenson's characteristically understated conclusion was:

"I think a rational person, if he wants, can believe in reincarnation on the basis of evidence."

And what about this thing with the birthmarks?

Well, take moles - technically known as hyperpigmented nevi – for instance. Although the average adult has between 15 and 19 of them, little is known about their cause and even less is known about why birthmarks occur in one location of the body instead of in another. In a few instances a genetic factor has been plausibly suggested for the location of nevi, but the cause of the location of most birthmarks remains unknown. More in general, the causes of many, perhaps most, birth defects remain similarly unknown. In large series of birth defects in which investigators have searched for the known causes, such as exposure to chemical substances, viral infections, and genetic factors, about two thirds of cases have finally been assigned to the category of "unknown causes."

And?

And Prof. Stevenson considered 895 cases of children who claimed to remember a previous life (or were thought by adults to have had a previous life), and found birthmarks and/or birth defects attributed to the previous life in 309 (35%) of the subjects. The birthmark or birth defect of the child was said to correspond to a wound (usually fatal) or other mark on the deceased person whose life the child said it remembered. Stevenson thoroughly investigated 210 of such cases. When he was able to identify the deceased person, he would carry out almost a police investigation, collecting all available information from a large number of sources and finding strong correlations in most cases. Whenever possible, he would even try to obtain a medical document, usually a postmortem report. He was able to do so in 49 cases, and *in 43 of those he found an almost stunning correspondence between wounds and birthmarks or birth defects.*

Moreover, although some of the birthmarks occurring on these children were ordinary hyperpigmented nevi, most were not. Instead, they were more likely to be puckered and scarlike, sometimes depressed a little below the surrounding skin, areas of hairlessness, areas of markedly diminished pigmentation (hypopigmented macules), or port-wine stains (nevipammri). When a relevant birthmark was a hyperpigmented nevus, it was nearly always larger in area than the ordinary mole. Similarly, the birth defects in these cases were of unusual types and rarely corresponded to any of the "recognizable patterns of human malformation" as described by Smith in 1982.

Can you give some examples.

Sure. Take for example a Thai boy, who remembered the life of a man who was shot with a rifle from behind. Prof. Stevenson was able to track down the identity of the man, and to get hold of a copy of the autopsy report. As you would expect, the autopsy spoke of a small entry hole at the back of the skull of the victim, and of a larger and irregular exit hole in the frontal area.

Stevenson was readily able to identify a small, round puckered birthmark on the back of the boy's head, and a larger, irregularly shaped birthmark on the frontal area.

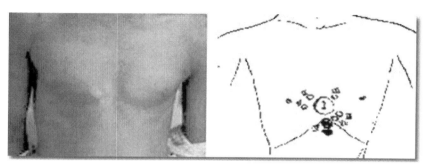

Another interesting story is that of one Indian youth who was born with a large area of his chest with no pigmentation. As a child, he claimed to remember a former life where he was a man named Maha Ram, a name otherwise unknown to him or the family, who was killed by a shotgun fired at close range. Prof. Stevenson was able to confirm that one Maha Ram was indeed shot shortly before the youth was born, and could get hold of the autopsy report. He asked a local pathologist to draw a sketch of the wounds as described in the autopsy report. The circles show the principal shotgun wounds on Maha Ram, when you compare them with the Indian youth the similarity is quite astounding.

In other cases, Stevenson found almost absent fingers (brachydactyly) on one hand in a boy of India who said he remembered the life of a boy of another village who had put his hand into the blades of a fodder chopping machine and had its fingers amputated…

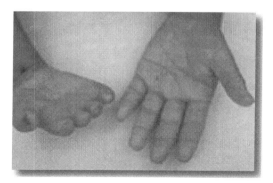

...or a severely malformed ear (microtia) in a Turkish boy who said that he remembered the life of a man who was fatally wounded on the right side of the head by a shotgun discharged at close range.

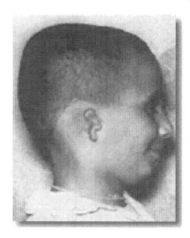

Very, very intriguing...

I know, but remember – these pictures are *nothing*. You cannot even begin to understand the weight of the evidence without taking a serious, close look at the work of Prof. Stevenson. *All* possible explanations are considered and thoroughly investigated, for every single case. The sheer amount of work that's gone into this... It's incredible. So, again, if you can't spend months going through all the published research, you are left with two alternatives - either you believe that a top-level academic spent an entire lifetime creating and keeping a colossal deception alive (and managing, in the process, to be consistently published in the scientific press without *ever* drawing any criticism by his peers), or you're looking at a white fly the size of a cow.

Yes, I know... Back to the memories, I understand that Prof. Stevenson did not use what they call "regressive hypnosis" to bring them back

Yes you are right. That is a field of research championed by Dr. Brian Weiss. The guy is another very interesting fellow, one that is really hard to dismiss as "intellectually weak and easily deluded". He graduated Phi Beta Kappa, magna cum laude, from Columbia University and got a PhD from Yale Medical School and serves today as Chairman Emeritus of

Psychiatry at Mount Sinai Medical center in Miami, Florida.

After earning his PhD and opening his own practice, Dr. Weiss went on for years as a traditional psychotherapist, with the kind of scientific conservative attitude that you would expect by a product of the scientific establishment. Things were to change in 1980, though, when he met a 27-year old patient, Catherine, who came to his office seeking help for her anxiety, panic attacks, and phobias. For 18 months, Dr. Weiss used conventional methods of treatment to help Catherine overcome her traumas. When nothing seemed to work, he tried hypnosis, which, he explains,

> "...is an excellent tool to help a patient remember long-forgotten incidents. There is nothing mysterious about it. It is just a state of focused concentration. Under the instruction of a trained hypnotist, the patient's body relaxes, causing the memory to sharpen... eliciting memories of long-forgotten traumas that were disrupting their lives."

During the initial sessions, the doctor regressed her back to her early childhood and she strained and stretched her mind bringing out isolated, deeply-repressed memory fragments. She remembered from age five when she swallowed water and felt gagged when pushed from a diving board into a pool; and at age three when her father reeking of alcohol molested her one night. But, when Dr. Weiss thought of going further back into Catherine's past, he was astonished to see her, in a series of trance-like states, recall "past life" memories that were to prove to be the causative factors of her recurring nightmares and anxiety attack symptoms. During months of therapy, she remembered living 86 times in physical state in different places on this earth, both as male and female. She recalled vividly the details of each birth – her name, her family, physical appearance, the landscape, and how she passed away.

As you would expect, despite the evident clinical progress, Dr. Weiss was highly skeptical of what Catherine was reporting. His skepticism, though, was to receive a serious blow when she began to channel messages from "the space between lives" - messages from disincarnate intelligences that contained shockingly accurate knowledge about his family and his dead son, that Catherine could obviously not have acquired directly.

This amazing story is told with wit by Dr. Weiss himself in his bestseller book *Many Lives, Many Masters* (Simon and Schuster, New York, 1988). Since then, Brian Weiss has successfully treated and documented hundreds of similar cases, pioneering an approach which is being followed by a number of researchers and clinicians around the world.

Yes – I had heard of the book.

There are several others by the same author that are worth reading. Now, I would like to end today's conversation with the extraordinary story I promised to tell you earlier. It's a beautiful story, not connected with Prof. Stevenson's work, but which I hope will help me conveying the sense of bewilderment that arises when studying his work. I can see no better way than to report to you the story as I learnt it myself, told by Tibetan Buddhist master Sogyal Rinpoche in his *Tibetan Book of Living and Dying* (HarperCollins, 2002).

"Of the hundreds of stories about reincarnation that could be told here, there is one that particularly fascinates me. It is the story of an elderly man from Norfolk in England called Arthur Flowerdew, who from the age of twelve experienced inexplicable but vivid mental pictures of what seemed like some great city surrounded by desert. One of the images that came most frequently to his mind was of a temple apparently carved out of a cliff. These strange images kept coming back to him, especially when he played with pink and orange pebbles on the seashore near his home. As he grew older, the details of the city in his vision grew clearer, and he saw more buildings, the layout of the streets, soldiers, and the approach to the city through a narrow canyon.

Arthur Flowerdew much later in his life, quite by chance, saw a television documentary film on the ancient city of Petra in Jordan. He was astounded to see, for the very first time, the place he had carried around for so many years in those pictures in his mind. He claimed afterward that he had never even seen a book about Petra. However, his visions became well known, and an appearance in a BBC television program brought him to the attention of the Jordanian government, who proposed to fly him to Jordan along with a BBC producer to film his reactions to Petra. His only previous trip abroad had been a brief visit to the French coast.

Before the expedition left, Arthur Flowerdew was introduced to a world authority on Petra and author of a book on the ancient city, who questioned him in detail, but was baffled by the precision of his knowledge, some of which he said could only been known by an archaeologist specializing in this area. The BBC recorded Arthur

Flowerdew's pre-visit description of Petra, so as to compare it with what would be seen in Jordan. Flowerdew singled out three places in his vision of Petra: a curious volcano-shaped rock on the outskirt of the city, a small temple where he believed he had been killed in the first century B.C., and an unusual structure in the city which was well known to archaeologists but for which they could find no function. The Petra expert could recall no such rock and doubted that it was there. When he showed Flowerdew a picture of the part of the city where the temple had stood, he astounded him by pointing to almost the exact site. Then the elderly man calmly explained the purpose of the structure, one that had not been considered before, as the guard room in which he served as a soldier two thousand years before.

A significant number of his predictions were accurate. On the expedition's approach to Petra, Arthur Flowerdew pointed out the mysterious rock; and once in the city, he went straight to the guard room, without a glance at the map, and demonstrated how its peculiar check-in system for guards was used. Finally, he went to the spot where he said he had been killed by an enemy spear in the first century B.C. He also indicated the location and purpose of other unexcavated structures on the site.

The expert and archaeologist of Petra who accompanied Arthur Flowerdew could not explain this very ordinary Englishman's uncanny knowledge of the city. He said:

He's filled in details and a lot of it is very consistent with known archaeological and historical facts and it would require a mind very different from his to be able to sustain a fabric of deception on the scale of his memories – at least those he's reported to me. I don't think he's a fraud. I don't think he has the capacity to be a fraud on this scale."

Day 14 - Poltergeist

These experiments were really a challenge to physics. What we saw in the Rosenheim case could be 100 per cent shown not to be explainable by known physics.

Dr. Friedbert Karger, Max Plank Institute

Poltergeist?

Yes.

As in the Hollywood *B movies*?

No.

What, then?

More white flies. As big and puzzling as anything we've considered so far.

Like what?

Like the pamphlet printed in London in 1698 by Mr. Ricard Chamberlain, which provides an account of a poltergeist-type haunting that had occurred some years before. Two copies of the pamphlet exist in the British Museum called: "Lithobolia, or stone throwing Devil. Being an Exact and True account (by way of Journal) of the various actions of infernal Spirits or (Devils Incarnate) Witches or both: and the great Disturbance and Amazement they gave to George Walton's family at a place called Great Island in the province of New Hampshire in New England, chiefly in throwing about (by an Invisible hand) Stones, Bricks, and Brick-Bats of all sizes, with several other things, as Hammers, Mauls, Iron-Crows, Spits, and other Utensils, as came into their Hellish minds, and this for space of a quarter of a year...."

1698?

A few years before Hollywood.

Quite so. As usual, then, let's start from the beginning...

Good idea. *Poltergeist* is a German word that roughly translates into "noisy spirit" and denotes a spirit or ghost that manifests itself by moving or influencing objects. During the last century, several mechanisms have been put forward by parpsychologists to try to explain the origins of these widespread and well documented phenomena.

First, noting that poltergeist activity often occurs around a single person called an agent or a focus, after almost seventy years of research, the Rhine Research Center in Raleigh-Durham, North Carolina, has proposed that the "poltergeist effect" could be a form of psychokinesis generated by a living human mind (that of the agent) as the outward manifestation of psychological trauma.

This explanation, however, does take into account neither the fact that – as we have already noted some days ago – PK effects are known to be quite small (whilst poltergeist activity is macroscopic), nor the fact that some poltergeist activities are not associated with any identifiable agent.

Another version has it that poltergeists originate after a person dies in a state of rage. According to yet another opinion, ghosts and poltergeists are "recordings." When there is a powerful emotion, sometimes at death and sometimes not, a recording is believed to be "embedded" in a place or, somehow, in the "fabric of time" itself. This recording will continue to play over and over again until the energy embedded disperses.

You will appreciate that such theories are really far-fetched, quite unscientific. Researchers are completely in the dark and simply try to make sense of the things they see. The most interesting thing, however, is that some poltergeists appear to have the ability to articulate themselves and to have distinct personalities, which suggests some sort of self-awareness and intent. This would support the survival hypothesis.

Umm...

Well – I understand your skepticism, but give me time to present some of the evidence and you'll perhaps understand. First, let's look at a very well known (and extremely well researched) case involving an agent.

The events took place in a city called Rosenheim in southern Bavaria, Germany, more specifically in the office of lawyer Sigmund Adam. Starting in 1967, strange phenomena began to manifest in the office - the lights would turn themselves off and on again, the phones would ring without anybody apparently calling, photocopiers spilled their copier fluid, objects would fly around and desk drawers would open without being touched. Not long after the onset of the inexplicable phenomena, the Deutsche Post was requested to investigate the anomalous behaviour of the phones and installed instruments that recorded numerous phone calls that were never made: within five weeks the instruments recorded roughly 600 calls to the speaking clock even though all the phones in the office were disabled and only Adam himself had the key required to enable them. In October 1967 all light bulbs went out with a huge bang.

The police, the electric company and others tried to find an explanation for all this for weeks, until they gave up with no useful explanation. A team of scientists, including the renowned parapsychologist Hans Bender and two Max Planck Institute physicists began investigating the case.
After installing cameras and voice recorders they were able to discover that the phenomena only occurred when 19-year old Annemarie Schneider (a recently employed secretary) was present. You can see her in the left picture, looking at a dish flying in mid air (you can make it out if you look just below the shelf on the wall). In the right picture, you can see one of the researchers pointing at a flying pen. On top of ample photographic evidence, Bender was able *to document on video how the lights immediately*

started to flicker once she entered the office and how a lamp shade would swing violently when Ms Schneider walked beneath it.

After questioning Ms Schneider, they found out that she was going through a difficult time due to a personal relationship turned wrong. Once the secretary was sent on vacation the poltergeist activity stopped. Annemarie Schneider was dismissed from the company when the infestations began anew after she had returned from her vacation. There are no records of any further infestations after that.

Interesting, as usual. What did critics say?

The usual things. That "the incident of all the lights blowing may suffer from some degree of exaggeration and is hardly unusual", that lights may well flicker in case of changes in the voltage, that desk drawers "often appear to roll out on their own, especially when the desk is sat on imperfect flooring" and that "photocopiers are hardly unknown to be unreliable". Also, we only have Adam's word that he held the only key to the phone system and – critics say – he may well be telling the truth, but "a trouble maker in the office (potentially the centre of the disturbances, Ms Schneider) may have made a surreptitious copy".

Let me be frank here. Personally, I think all that is nonsense. "Rational" explanations may account for the isolated freak accident, but thinking that such an incredible cluster of inexplicable events would occur over a relatively short time span by chance is – as I said – nonsense.

And so?

So, like in many other cases, the only explanation that I consider realistic is fraud. And, once more, I leave it up to your own judgment. Think of the motives of Ms Schneider – what would she stand to gain? Remember that she was even dismissed… And think: could she organize all this by herself? Impossible, isn't it? She should enlist her lawyer employer, and the other colleagues in the law firm. And all that conspiracy should be able to fool for weeks on end the police, the phone company, the electricity company, plus two physicists from an institution that the *Times Higher Education Supplement* ranked number 1 in the world in 2006 among non-university research centres. Before stopping for a moment to reflect, re-consider the quote from one of them, Dr. Karger, that I gave you in the beginning.

Now we can turn to another quite extraordinary story, which appears to involve a "distinct personality Poltergeist" and, as I said earlier, adds to the load of evidence in support of the survival hypothesis. First, however, I have to introduce you to whom I consider *the* single most important personality we'll encounter in our conversations.

Professor David Fontana is a Ph.D. in psychology, and is currently Distinguished Visiting Fellow at Cardiff University in South Wales, Great Britain, and Professor of Transpersonal Psychology at Liverpool John Moores University, also in Great Britain. In addition he has held invited professorships at the Universities of Minho and of Algarve in Portugal. He is a Fellow of the British Psychological Society, a Chartered Psychologist and a Chartered Counselling Psychologist and the author of 26 books on psychology translated into 25 languages. I consider Professor Fontana so important because one of his books (*Is There an Afterlife? A Comprehensive Review of the Evidence*, O Books, 2005) is the first (and could well have been the only) book I ever read on the subject. In the book (a hefty 575 pages), Prof. Fontana, who is a long standing member of the Society for Psychical Research, for which he served as Chairman of the Survival Committee, demonstrates an absolutely encyclopedic knowledge of the subject and a cautious, open-minded skeptic attitude that wins the reader over from the very first pages.

As you would expect, *Is There An Afterlife?* devotes one chapter to Poltergeist. Much of the chapter is used by Prof. Fontana to provide an account of the absolutely stunning three-month investigation he was asked to carry out at a very ordinary location – a workshop for the repair of lawnmowers adjacent to a gardening shop in Cardiff, Wales, UK.

The account begins with Fontana arriving at the workshop for the first time. Upon entering it, he sees the owner, John Matthews, and a visiting salesman. The salesman is sitting on some low boxes with his hands on his knees, whereas John Matthews is standing near some machinery when all of a sudden, even before the Professor could introduce himself, a loud 'ping' is heard as a stone, apparently materialized in flight out of thin air, hits the machinery. Mr. Matthews does not appear to be fazed at all by the projectile and even calmly said to Fontana "There you are, he's welcoming you."

John Matthews and the salesman went on to tell Fontana that even though they were originally skeptical, they had seen enough for them to believe that something paranormal was behind it all. Matthews had become so used to the activity, he had even named the unseen force 'Pete'.

Matthews told Fontana that the activity had started with Pete throwing large stones onto the roof of a shed in which John and one of his workmen were watching rugby one Saturday afternoon. Since then, the stone throwing had become so frequent that the police were called in on a number of occasions to catch the suspected culprits who, at the time, were thought to be some of the local youths. So far the police had been unable to find anyone responsible.

Mr. Matthews told Fontana that odd things had occurred inside the workshop too, including stones, bolts and even coins being thrown against the walls or being found scattered about the floor. If this was not enough, objects were said to fall from the ceiling or just appear on the work surfaces, such as pens, keys and coins. Tools were said to swing for no apparent reason; a blue case had been thrown violently around the room and planks of wood that are far too heavy to be thrown by hand had been hurtled through the open door of the workshop.

Mrs. Matthews, whilst sitting on the toilet, had stones thrown at the toilet door, dust had been stuffed down Mr. Matthews collar and loud knocks had been heard coming from the windows even when no one had been visible outside. Most frequent of all was the movement of small floats used in the carburetors of the lawnmowers in the workshop for repair.

Was this activity associated to any person in particular?

Good question. No, such events took place when John Matthews was in the workshop as well as when he was away and seemed to be totally random in nature. At some stage, during the investigation, the entire family went away on holiday, and the phenomena showed no change in size or frequency.

What was the investigation like?

Well, first of all, Fontana was himself a witness of a great number of the phenomena described by Matthews and others. One day, for example, Matthews told Fontana that he was getting frustrated by Pete because he kept throwing stones around the workshop and so he decided to throw one back into the corner of the room where most of the events originated. Within seconds of him throwing the stone into the corner, the very same stone came flying back at him and struck a wall near him. John repeated this again and it happened again!

The very next day Fontana tried the same experiment and reports in his own words:

> "I tried my own hand at stone throwing, again from twenty feet away and aiming into the same corner of the workshop, and to my surprise a stone was returned, hitting the wall behind me. I tried again with the same result. Over the following days and weeks John, Pat (Mrs Matthews) and I spent much time in the stone throwing game. Sometimes we got results, sometimes we were ignored. Nothing happened if we threw stones elsewhere in the workshop. Only one corner, which we named the active corner, prompted a response."

According to Fontana and other witnesses, these stones were never seen in flight but a ping and a clatter could be heard as the stone hit the wall and bounced onto the floor.

On another occasion, Matthews challenged Pete – apparently good at materializing things out of nothing – to materialize some cash. Fontana witnessed three pennies from 1912 being produced in a few minutes. Matthews then told Pete that pennies were not good enough, and he should produce some real money. *In the following weeks almost one hundred five Pounds notes were to appear in the workshop!*

Needless to say, Fontana took considerable pain to eliminate any possibility of fraud. He checked extensively the workshop, the adjacent shop and the house, paying particular attention that there were no concealed cupboards in the walls, ceiling or floors and made sure that there were no hidden accomplices. More importantly, he carried out dozens of interviews with the people involved, with customers of the workshop, with neighbors and acquaintances. This was crucial, as he could find no *motives* for fraud. Mr. Matthews himself was worried about the impact this could potentially have on his business as it was not unknown for Pete to frighten customers. In the end Fontana believed Mr. Matthews and the other witnesses to be honest, reliable and trustworthy people who disliked publicity but were simply perplexed by the paranormal phenomena that they had been a witness to.

Could it not be said, though, that Fontana, having a keen interest in psychic research, was a biased investigator? That he wanted to find something, he wanted things to fit with his world view?
One could. But then you have to remember two things. First, Fontana investigated the case on behalf of the SPR. We have encountered the Society already in our conversation, and you will remember that it is a conservative organization, which demands the highest scientific and integrity standards of its members.

Second, you have to remember that Fontana is primarily a scientist. He addresses these concerns himself in his book, in a very personal way, when he describes what he called 'morning after skepticism'. He would witness strange phenomena at the lawnmower workshop and leave for the night totally convinced that what he had witnessed was indeed paranormal. But then his analytical mind would take over again, and he would convince himself over night that it *had* to be related to a reasonable rational explanation. The morning after, however, his skepticism, which had regained strength overnight, was to be dealt additional blows.

When the stones were thrown into the corner of the workshop, for instance, he recounts how it would be logical to assume that the stones that were being returned were simply the original stones thrown, simply bounced back off the wall. However, he was astonished to note that the stones that were being returned were *not* the stone that he just threw into the corner. If that was not enough, in another incident Fontana asked Pete to hit a WWII 25lb brass shell case that Mr. Matthews kept in the workshop as a souvenir. As soon as he asked Pete to hit it, a loud ping was heard from the shell case as a stone ricocheted off it. Fontana tried and failed himself to hit the shell case, but then he asked Pete to help him out and his next shot hit the target.

At the end of three months of careful investigation, Fontana reported back to the SPR stating:

> "In sum, I am in no doubt that it would be very difficult for even the most determined critic to fall back on the argument of fraud at any point during my period of investigation. I was extremely fortunate in witnessing so many phenomena myself and in the company of individuals of whose integrity I had plenty of time and opportunity to satisfy myself."

Day 15 - Cross-correspondences

The most convincing proof of the reality of life after death ever set down on paper.
Colin Wilson

Today, we shall look at "historic" evidence for the last time. From tomorrow, it'll be all contemporary stuff, controlled experimental conditions and laboratory findings. Prepare yourself, however, because we're in for a really tough one!

Why are you saying that?

Because it will be tough for you to follow me. I'll need your full attention and concentration. And, I have to admit, it'll be really tough for me to talk to you about cross-correspondences in a way that does justice to what many consider as the Holy Grail of the survival hypothesis. I could have just explained to you the concept – which in itself is not especially complicated – and told you that the evidence around it is enormous and has been thoroughly researched and analyzed for almost 100 years, and that the results are, as in other cases we've seen, stunning.

Instead, as I did in the past, I want to provide you with sufficient information for you to form your own judgment. But what is "sufficient information" on such an incredibly deep and complex subject? How to select? How to try to explain?

Why don't you start from some definitions? Tell me what "cross-correspondences" means...

No, I thought of that, but I'd rather try to work our way to definitions – and, ultimately, understanding – in a more participatory way, starting from the periphery and gradually moving towards the centre. Let me start by introducing the key character of this complicated story.

Frederic Myers was born in 1843 and was educated at Cheltenham and at Trinity College, Cambridge, where he excelled academically, and in 1865 was appointed classical lecturer. He authored several poems and essays, one of which (*Essays, Classical and Modern*, 1883) is considered a major scholarly achievement. Myers' intellectual curiosity, however, went far beyond the study of Greek and Latin literature. He felt that if human life did have a purpose, then it could be discovered in only one way: through the study of human experiences. This conviction led him, in 1882, to found the Society for Psychical Research with some of his Cambridge colleagues. He contributed greatly to the coherence of the Society by steering a mid-course between extremes (the extreme skepticism on the one hand, and the enthusiastic spiritualists on the other), and by sifting and revising for years the large mass of the Society's *Proceedings*. After twenty years of intensive investigation, he wrote a book about what he had learned that became a classic - probably the most important work ever written in this field - called *Human Personality and Its Survival of Bodily Death*.

Now that you have an idea of who he was, try for a moment to put yourself in Frederic Myers' shoes. If you've been so passionate about psychic research and you are convinced that human personality survives physical death, what would you do if you actually found yourself somehow alive after having left this world?

I would probably try to communicate with the living.

Is that all?

Yes, I think so. What more can there be?

Well, think of having battled for years with the obtuse skeptics on one side and with the overenthusiastic on the other. Think of having looked left, right and centre for that elusive proof that would have demonstrated conclusively, beyond any possible doubt what you *knew* it was true...

Oh, I see what you mean. I would like to try to provide a watertight proof that I exist as a disincarnate personality.

Very good! Here we have the first element of the complex puzzle we're going to describe: we will call this element "the communicator", and by that we'll refer to Frederic Myers (and others, but we'll concentrate on him in today's conversation), who wanted to prove that he still exists as a disincarnate personality after his death, which, by the way, occurred in 1901.
Now – if that was your desire, how would you try to do that?

By communicating something very special, something that would make me recognisable as myself. Possibly something that only I would know.

That's good thinking, but, as we have seen in previous days, all that happens regularly in the communication from the Spirit world, and still the hardline skeptics are not convinced. Just remember the *super-psi* hypothesis, for instance...

The one that maintains that mediums read the information in the sitters' minds?

Yes, that one. Or the other theory that says that mediums in fact read memories somehow imprinted into some sort of *field*... Remember that Myers wanted to prove that his personality not only survived, but was still capable of interacting with this side of life in a conscious way.

Ummm... I am lost. I have no idea.

Fine. Let's leave this for the moment, because Myers' astute answer to this problem was exactly the cross-correspondences, which we'll arrive at later. Now, we have to introduce another element of the puzzle, which we'll refer to as "the automatic writers".

I think I've heard enough so far to be able to guess. Automatic writing is another form of communication through mediums: communicators induce mediums to write instead of speaking.

Very, very good! Automatic writers enter into a light trance and write large quantities of material, often in a handwriting that's not their own and sometimes in languages they don't know. Our story involves a group of mediums, most of whom were automatic writers, operating in three continents during the first three decades of the last century.

In the group, the only professional medium was Mrs. Eleanore Piper (far right in the picture), working and living in the US, whom we've already met in the early days of our conversations. At this stage, it is critical that you appreciate that Mrs. Piper was of average education and had no knowledge of the classics, let alone of Greek or Latin language. In the UK, three main characters and a few minor ones are involved in the story. There is a Mrs. and a Ms. Verral, mother and daughter (at the center of the picture), both highly educated, the mother being herself a lecturer in classics at Cambridge, one Mrs Salter, also well-educated and with a good knowledge of Latin and Greek literature, and one Mrs. Willett. Relatively minor characters include one Mrs Forbes and one Mrs Wilson. Finally, we have the sister of Rudyard Kipling (left in the picture), who lived in India and whom we know under the pseudonym of Mrs Holland, as her husband and family strongly disapproved of her psychic activities.

Then, an additional element of the puzzle is what we'll call "the gatherer". By that, we refer to Alice Johnson, who served many years as Research Officer for the SPR.

Finally, we have "the scholars". That includes mainly J.E. Piddington, former Honorary Secretary of the SPR; Gerald Balfour, a prominent political figure, who served as Prime Minister and Foreign Secretary; Sir Oliver Lodge; and Mrs. Sidgwick, wife of another founder of the SPR. Crucially, on top of their interest for psychic research, most of these people had a good knowledge of the classics.

Hold on a minute – I'm getting confused already. We've talked of "the communicator", "the automatic writers", "the gatherer" and "the scholars", right?

Yes, right. Let's try to piece the puzzle together, then, and provide a simplified description of the mechanism of the cross-correspondences.

1) Within a few weeks of Myers' death in 1901, some very strange communications began to be received by the automatic writers in England, the United States and India.

2) These communications – known as "scripts" – made no sense to the reader and certainly not to the automatic writers themselves. Many of them would be cryptic, arcane, often with allusions to the classics. They were so mysteriously worded that it almost seemed their meaning was being deliberately concealed.

3) The scripts, however, were often signed "Myers" and contained clear instructions: they should be sent to a particular person, who would turn out to be one of the other automatic writers involved, or it should be sent to the "gatherer", Alice Johnson of the Society for Psychical Research in London. These instructions and explanations were, in fact, frequent and explicit. "Record the bits," wrote 'Myers' through one of the mediums, "and when fitted they will make the whole." And again, "I will give the words between you that neither alone can read but together they will give the clue."

4) And this is exactly what happened. When the scripts started to amass in London, the "scholars" (Piddington, initially, and the others soon later) started analyzing them as a whole and discovered a clear, coherent literary fresco, of such a size and spectacular complexity that its study was a lifetime occupation for all of them.

So, these are the cross-correspondences: bits of communication that make no sense on their own but make sense when analyzed together?

Exactly! But you have to appreciate that this went on for thirty years, and the scripts known as cross-correspondences amount to over twelve thousand pages!

Wow!

Good. Now pay even more attention, as we have to look at least at some examples in the ocean of extraordinary evidence provided by the cross-correspondences. I would like to begin with what is now known as the *Sevens cum Dante Case*, which was spread over a period of four and a half years, but with a surge of activity between 20 April and 24 July 1908. Seven persons were involved in this particular case: six automatic writers and one scholar – J.E. Piddington.

The case begins at the Society's room in London, with Piddington himself who, on the morning of 13 of July 1904, wrote a "posthumous letter" (that is, a letter that should have been opened after his death), sealed it and handed it to the gatherer – Alice Johnson – to keep. The letter began as follows:

"If ever I am a spirit, and if I can communicate, I shall endeavour to remember to transmit in some form or other the number SEVEN. As it seems to me not improbable that it may be difficult to transmit an exact word or idea, it may be that, unable to transmit the simple word seven in writing or as a written number, 7, I should try to communicate such things as: 'The seven lamps of architecture', 'The seven sleepers of Ephesus', 'unto seventy times seven', 'We are seven', and so forth. The reason why I select the word seven is because seven has been a kind of tic with me ever since my early boyhood..."

He continues by referring to his habit of taking it as a good omen for his golf if he saw from the links a railway engine drawing seven carriages, and added that he had purposely cultivated "this tic", as the memory of it might "survive the shock of death". You still with me?

Yes. A posthumous letter with indications concerning number seven. And a tic.

Good. But careful now – remember that the communicator is Myers, not Piddington. As the Sevens Case unfolds, Piddington is alive and well, whilst Myers has been in spirit since 1901.

Why are you stressing that?

Because within minutes from Piddington writing his posthumous letter, precisely at 11.15 a.m. Mrs. Verrall, who was then in Surrey, wrote a script which, after some nonsensical Latin and Greek words, continued:

"It is something contemporary that you are to record - note the hour - in London half the message has come."

The rest of the script purports to give the contents of Myers's posthumous envelope and ends:

"Surely Piddington will see that this is enough and should be acted on. F.W.H.M."

F.W.H.M.?

These are the initials of Myers name. He signed his communications through the automatic writers either as "Myers" or with the initials.

This would mean, then, that Myers, who had been dead three years, was aware of Piddington writing the letter and communicated this through one of the automatic writers?

It would appear so... Then, nothing more happened for over three years. On the 6 August 1907 Helen Verrall (daughter of the Mrs. Verrall who received the first communication) wrote:

"A rainbow in the sky
   fit emblem of our thought
The sevenfold radiance from a single light
   many in one and one in many."

The script continued with a Latin sentence, which might be construed as meaning that someone had sent messages to various persons, and that these messages were to be "coordinated".

On 28 August 1907, Mrs. Verrall wrote a script including these words:

"Try this new experiment - Say the same sentence to each of them and see what completion each gives to it. Let Piddington choose a sentence that they do not know and send part to each. Then see whether they can complete".

The case really begins to become intricate when Piddington discovered, on 15 February 1908, that a script written by Mrs. Holland on 8 April 1907 was a reference to a passage of Dante's *Divina Commedia*, and in particular an account of Canto 27 of the *Purgatorio*.

These allusions seemed to throw light on a number of other references to Dante in the scripts of the other automatic writers, including Mrs. Piper in the US (who, as we already noted, had no knowledge of the classics). Piddington also discovered that allusions to the *Divina Commedia* were closely connected in the scripts with allusions to seven. Just allow me to remind you that that in Canto 27 Dante speaks of a dream he had whilst in the Seventh Circle, and then, in Canto 28 he, Vergil and Statius reach a flowery meadow through which runs a small stream. Following this towards the sunrise (Canto 29) they see approaching seven candlesticks, the flames of which leave in the heavens a trail of the colours of the rainbow. Read again what Helen Verrall wrote six months before:

"A rainbow in the sky
   fit emblem of our thought
The sevenfold radiance from a single light
   many in one and one in many."

Well she could have taken that from the *Commedia* herself...

First, it turns out that Helen was not familiar with the *Purgatorio*: she read the Cantos only in May 1908, after Piddington had informed her of the multiple allusions. Second – why that particular section of the gigantic *Divina Commedia*? Why the allusions to number seven?

I see.

Hold on - let's continue with the following scripts, as we are entering in the paroxysm of this case. On 8 May Mrs. Piper in America, during the waking-stage that followed her trance, said "Ye are Seven. I said Clock! Tick, tick, tick." Do you remember? "We are seven" is one of the phrases Piddington mentioned in his posthumous letter, and "tick, tick, tick" may well allude to the tic that Piddington twice speaks of.

On 11 May 1908, six thousand kilometres away, Helen Verrall wrote a script including references to a) Jacob's ladder, b) a spinning top with many colours that blend into one, c) the seven-branched candlestick and the seven colours of the rainbow, and the words "many mystic sevens... we are seven." The script is signed "F. W. H. Myers".

On 12 May 1908 Mrs. Piper gave a sitting at which Dorr, the American investigator, asked her to explain some of the words she had spoken on 8 May, including "We are seven". She wrote "We *were* seven in the distance as a matter of fact" and, after questions on other subjects, "Seven of us, 7, seven".

On 11 June Mrs. Frith wrote a poem including the following lines:

"Pisgah is scaled the fair and dewy lawn
Invites my footsteps till the mystic seven
Lights up the golden candlestick of dawn."

On 23 July 1908 Mrs. Holland, then at sea, wrote:

"There should be at least three in accord and if possible seven."

She proceeds to describe symbolically the seven who should be in accord, specifying six of the actual seven correctly, but leaving out Piddington and apparently including a minor automatist, Mrs. Forbes, who was not in fact concerned.

On 24 July 1908 'Myers', purporting to speak through Mrs. Home, said

"Seven times seven and seventy-seven send the burden of my words to others".

The drama draws towards conclusion in November 1908. On the 19th Alice Johnson told Piddington that she herself had noticed a sevens cross-correspondence with Dante allusions in the scripts of Mrs. Verrall, Helen Verrall, Mrs. Holland, Mrs. Piper, Mrs. Frith and Mrs. Home. On the 27th, after he and she had examined the case more thoroughly, he told her that the subject of his posthumous letter was variations on the theme of Seven. She then got out the sealed envelope from the locked drawer where she had kept it. They examined it, found the seals intact and opened it. Until that day she had had no inkling what the contents might be.

On 27 January 1909 Mrs. Verrall, who did not even know that such an envelope existed, wrote a script ending with the following passage:

"And ask what has been the success of Piddington's last experiment? Has he found the bits of his famous sentence scattered among you all? And does he think that is accident, or started by one of you? But even if the source is human, who carries the thoughts to the receivers? Ask him that. F.W.H.M."

Bingo.

Aye – bingo. Do you understand why I said that this would have been a tough day?

Yes, I do. Very complicated things. But I have to admit that the story is astounding.

Astounding it is indeed, but believe me – it's just one in literally dozens of similar examples amid the Myers cross-correspondences. The *Sevens cum Dante* looks intricate, but compared with other cases is really not. Another well-known and not too complicated example is the *Hope, Star and Browning Case*, where the words Star and Hope are repeatedly given, together with quotations from the poet Browning which his friends said were characteristic of Myers. These were given by both Mrs. and Miss Verrall, but they were only pulled together when Myers, communicating through Mrs Piper in America, indicated that he had completed a cross correspondence and gives the words Browning, Hope and Star as the clues.

The case started on 16 January 1907, when Mr. Piddington asked Myers (through Mrs. Piper) if in future he could indicate that a cross correspondence was being attempted by drawing, say a circle with a triangle inside. Naturally, he *did not* mention this request to the other automatists.

On 23 January Mrs Verrall wrote in her script:

"... an anagram would be better. Tell him that - rats, stars, tars and so on ... or again tears, stare."

This was followed by another anagram which Mrs Verrall afterwards remembered had also been devised during their lives by Myers, her husband and Sir Richard Jebb. Some time later, when Piddington was going through Richard Hodgson's papers - Hodgson died in 1905 - he found that Hodgson and Myers had been exchanging anagrams for years and that both the star anagram and the other quoted were among the papers.

On 28 January Mrs Verrall's 'Myers' set about elaborating the Star idea (Aster in Latin). He wrote:

"Teras [an anagram for Aster, occasionally used in Greek for a constellation and also meaning a wonder or a sign]. The world's wonder. And all a wonder and a wild desire. The very wings of her. A WINGED DESIRE. Hupopteros eros [Greek = winged love]. Then there is Blake. And mocked my loss of liberty. But it is all the same thing - the winged desire. Eros potheinos [Greek = love, the much desired] the hope that leaves the earth for the sky. That is what I want. On earth the broken sounds - threads - in the sky the perfect arc. The C major of this life. But your recollection is at fault."

After this was drawn:

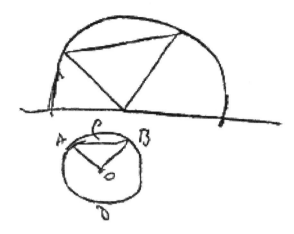

and the script concluded:

"ADB is the part that completes the arc."

Helen Verrall had not seen these scripts of her mother's but on February 3rd she wrote:

"... where the song birds pipe their tune in the early morning",

and followed this by

"Therapeutikos ek exoticon"[1] (a healer from aliens)

which was a veiled hint of what was to come later. Next came a monogram, the drawing of a star and a crescent moon and the words:

"A monogram, the crescent moon, remember that and the star."

Finally she drew a bird.

Can you please tell me what you picked up so far?

Umm... Let me think. First, the incredible drawing from Mrs Verrall: a circle with a triangle inside, exactly as Piddington had suggested. And then variations on the theme of star – anagrams and the drawings and specific references by Helen Verrall. "Winged love", "winged desire", "song birds" and the drawing of a bird. One only explicit reference to hope, though.

Excellent! And here's your "hope": on 11 February Mrs Piper's 'Myers' asked Piddington if Mrs. Verrall had received the word Evangelical. He answered that he did not know, and 'Myers' went on:

"I referred also to Browning again. I referred to Hope and Browning ... I also said Star."

Later on he said that the word Evangelical was wrong. He had meant to say Evelyn Hope (the title of a poem by Browning) but in transmission the words had been distorted into Evangelical.

Next came a nice touch. Miss Verrall had so far done comparatively little automatic writing and to stimulate and encourage her she was told that she had taken part in a cross correspondence which included the words Planet Mars, Virtue and Keats (a deliberate disguise of the real theme of the cross-correspondence). On 17 February , 'Myers' wrote through her:

"That was the sign. She will understand when she sees it ... No arts avail ... and a star above it all rats everywhere in Hamelin town."

Arts, star, rats...

Oh, yes, and by the mention of "rats everywhere in Hamelin Town", the script is linked to the earlier phrase, "The healer from aliens", which is an apt description of Browning's *Pied Piper of Hamelin*.

Wow...

Wait. On 6 March, Mrs. Piper's 'Myers' told Piddington that he had given Mrs. Verrall a circle. He then tried to draw a triangle, but commented: "It did not appear." This is an interesting mistake, as Mrs Verrall had in fact succeeded in drawing a triangle as well as a circle. He also said, correctly, that he had written something about Bird when he gave Mrs Verrall the circle.

On 13 March Mrs Piper's 'Myers' repeated that he had drawn a circle for Mrs Verrall and he again drew a circle and a triangle. Afterwards he said:

"But it suggested a poem to my mind, hence B H S."

(i.e. Browning, Hope, Star).

Finally, on 8 April Mrs Piper's 'Myers' once more repeated that he had drawn a circle for Mrs Verrall and added that he had also drawn or had tried to draw a star and a crescent. That these two symbols had been drawn was correct, but it had been Miss Verrall, not her mother, who had drawn them.

Mesmerizing...

Yes, indeed. Now, I need your attention for another couple of minutes. Rather than giving more examples (these two ones were easy, imagine the difficult ones...) I want to conclude by telling you about two ways that our scholar Piddington and an American researcher, G. B. Dorr devised to testing the cross-correspondences, as described in an article by Rosalyn Heywood:

The first was to try and check whether they could result from ordinary associations of ideas on the part of the automatists, the other to find out if their creators, whoever they were, would produce a cross correspondence to order. In the first test fourteen people were each sent quotations, twelve in all, from Shakespeare, Milton, Shelley, Rostand, Virgil, Wordsworth, Coleridge and Homer, and were asked to write down some words or phrases associated with them. The results were very different from the cross correspondences produced spontaneously by the automatists. Only momentary cross-references occurred and there was no tendency to return again and again to one master theme, in fact there was no resemblance at all to a real cross correspondence.

The next test was to set the purported 'Myers' a subject for a cross correspondence which would give scope for classical knowledge beyond that of most of the automatists. The plan was that in America Dorr should ask Mrs Piper's 'Myers' the question, "What does the word Lethe suggest to you?", Mrs Piper herself being no classical scholar. He did so and at several sittings he obtained in response a number of classical allusions which meant nothing to him and also nothing at first to the scholars of the British SPR. The allusions included Myers-like references to the little-known story of Ceyx and Alcyone and to the sending of the Goddess, Iris to the underworld as this is told in connection with the river Lethe in Ovid's Metamorphoses. Later on, Sir Oliver Lodge asked Mrs Willett's 'Myers' the same question. He answered that it had already been asked elsewhere, and with great effort spelled out the word DORR in capitals. Then, over a period of weeks, Mrs Willett's script made many allusions to references in Virgil's Aneid to the river Lethe and these fitted Mr Dorr's question from the point of view of such a man as Myers, who had known his Virgil inside out, but did not do so from that of people without his scholarship. Ultimately Mrs Willett's 'Myers' wrote:

"That I have different scribes means that I must show different aspects of thoughts underlying which Unity is to be found and I know what Lodge wants. He wants me to prove that I have access to knowledge shown elsewhere."

Finally, let's leave Frederic Myers and his cross-correspondences with a last, striking bit. In March 1910, Mrs Verrall wrote a series of scripts referring to the main events in the history of the City of Rome. On March 7th, *five thousand miles away*, Mrs Holland wrote:

"Ave Roma Immortalis. How could I make it clearer without giving her the clue?"

Day 16 - Energy-based phenomena

No testimony is sufficient to establish a miracle, unless the testimony be of such a kind, that its falsehood would be more miraculous than the fact which it endeavours to establish.

David Hume

Miracles – that's what we've come to now!

Yes, miracles that were featured on the front cover of The Sunday Times magazine, in the Daily Mail, in Time Out, in a number of Japanese, French, German, and American journals, on British TV and Radio and in a 2-hour documentary made in the US. And, as I will show to you in due course, miracles for which so much extraordinary testimony exists that falsehood is simply not an option.

Well, honestly, I must say that this applies to most of the things we've been discussing so far. By now, I have to admit that I have almost completely surrendered to the evidence you presented me with. I feel overwhelmed, and I am not sure of what else you can call "miracles"...

You make me laugh out loud here! And you are very right – it's difficult to believe that there's much more beyond what we've looked at already. The bad – or, rather, the *very good* – news is that this is indeed the case. We still have a few days of wonderment and amazement in stock, and today we start with the Scole experiment, which is extremely important for a number of reasons.

OK, then. I'll fasten my seat belts. What is Scole, and why is it so important?

The Scole Experiment takes its name from the Norfolk village where the most incredible series of séances took place during the early 1990's, and by the fact that it was indeed an experiment. Hold yourself tight, here. Apart from the quite extraordinary happenings and the extent of the scrutiny to which they were subject, Scole is regarded as crucially important because it clearly consisted of a *joint* experiment, carried out in collaboration by two teams (both including scientists) - one on this side, *and the other one on the spirit side.*

Away you go!

No, really, that's exactly what happened. In our conversation today I'll try to summarize for you the incredible variety of phenomena that were produced, but it's important that you understand that such phenomena grew in size and diversity over a period of roughly five years. This happened as the communicators on the spirit side continuously tried out and improved new techniques, and showed the researchers on this side on how to maximize the effects of the experiments, *including by giving detailed instructions on pieces of technical equipment to be built!*

For God's sake – this is more outlandish than a Hollywood movie!

I know, I know. It is indeed quite incredible. Also, another very important feature of the experiment is that an entirely new, "energy-based" (as opposed to ectoplasm-based) method was used to produce the most astonishing physical phenomena.

Now, to put things into perspective let me start – as I have done often – by talking about the people involved. I hope this will help to move away from the "Hollywood mindset"… Look at this picture, to begin with, and tell me what you see.

People.

People?

Yes, normal people, average folks. It could be a family reunion, or friends meeting for tea. They don't really look like big party goers, if you see what I mean...

Not the kind of people who would mount an extraordinarily elaborate deception during a period of over five years in order to reach world fame and great wealth?

Ummm... no, not really.

Exactly. They don't look like it, and in fact they're not. Rather, they're people who've put an inordinate amount of work into an experiment that has brought them absolutely no money – if anything, quite some expenses... – and very little personal fame outside the psychic research world. In fact, *the two mediums around which the experiment revolved remained anonymous at their own request for all those years,* and still today, after a report in the national press betrayed their confidence, we know very little about them apart from their names!

The picture shows the so-called Scole Group: on the left and right in the picture you see Robin Foy and his wife Sandra. On the centre you see the two mediums, who were later identified as Diana and Alan Bennett. Robin Foy, a sales manager, had been a passionate psychic researcher for all of his adult life, particularly dedicated to investigating physical mediumship, and it was in the cellar of his home at Scole (familiarly known as the "Scole hole") that the experiment took place.

I would like to let Robin set the stage and tell the story of the beginnings of the experiment, before scientists and researchers were involved.

"In the beginning, when the Scole group was first formed at the end of 1992, it seemed to be just another of our home circles to add to the many which Sandra and I had formed and run since we met in 1977 and married in 1979. We certainly had dedicated sitters. Two group members were prepared to drive 70 miles and back from their homes to Scole on a weekly basis in their own time and at their own expense. Although the phenomena we witnessed in the group were to be quite amazing, it took over six months of weekly sittings before any significant physical psychic phenomena occurred."

Hang on a second – he means that they sat in a dark cellar twice a week for six months before anything happened?

Welcome to the world of grassroots psychical research! See what Robin himself says.

"Yes, we did experience the usual coldness in the room that traditionally accompanies physical phenomena, and a few random raps and taps around the cellar of our home at Scole where the group sat, but nothing significant until May 1993 when, at one session, the trumpet which we had standing on the central table fell off the table onto the lap of a sitter.

The next week, the trumpet again levitated, but in a more controlled manner, before gently returning to the table top. Following this, there were several more months of relative inactivity where physical phenomena was concerned, although the time was used by the spirit team to introduce a few regular spirit helpers, speaking through the trance state of Diana and Alan Bennett, who went on to become our mediums for trance communication with the spirit team who worked with us.

During this 'lull' in the p..
as communicators becam..
Diana and Alan, the relation..
became very much a two-wa..
and mutual co-operation. At t..
communicators went out of the..
profusion of evidential message..
details not known by anyone else w..

It is generally acknowledged tha..
controlled phenomena associated wit..
October 1993, when only three of us w.. ..t
bed ill at that time). An apport of a 'Chu.. ..ceived
(this dropped loudly onto the central table .. ..ession), and
we were told that it was a sign of greater .. .. to come. What a
prophetic statement that subsequently proved to be!

Within weeks we witnessed several strong new instances of physical
psychic phenomena. Remember that at the beginning we had no
idea that these phenomena was being produced in a new way, and
assumed that ectoplasm was the basis of the spirit activity. Initially,
as we were later told by the spirit team, they made a great effort to
duplicate the types of phenomena that were produced in the more
traditional way For instance, in the first few weeks, we were treated
to an amazing display of trumpets flying round the room but - it
was done in such a way as to show us that the versatility of the
trumpet movements was greater than we had ever witnessed before.
This perplexed us, and set us wondering how on earth the trumpets
could weave through and around chair legs etc, as we knew that this
degree of flexibility during levitation was not normal when
ectoplasm was being used as, in the traditional way, the trumpets
were attached to a physical medium by means of an ectoplasmic
psychic rod, which limited their movement greatly.

Having therefore mystified us as to how the traditional type of
phenomena we were witnessing had been achieved, it was not long
before the regular communicators explained to us that this was a
pioneering set of experiments in physical psychic phenomena which
we were undertaking together, but which was using only a blend of
natural energies, itself producing a creative energy which could be
used by operatives in the spirit team to achieve their aims. Indeed,
on one occasion, Dr. Dunn, the spirit scientist associated with the
Romford circle in which Sandra and I met, came to the Scole group

...t that the energy now being used was
...us, issued back in the days of the Romford
...iier!

...grasped the principles of the new modus operandi, the
...development continued apace at an unprecedented rate.
...ail, but rapidly moving spirit lights became a regular feature of
the sessions, and we were told that these were originally not
intentional on the part of the spirit team, but were actually a by-
product of other work that the spirit team were undertaking. When
it was realised that the lights were visible to us, and that they caused
much excitement, then the lights, too, were developed, till they
became a permanent feature of the sessions, and were witnessed by
hundreds of guests in all during our demonstrations and seminars
which took place at a later date.

As the group progressed, many and varied were the different types
of phenomena that were developed and demonstrated to us by the
spirit helpers. Over the years, the actual number of types of physical
phenomena ran to almost 200 - a fantastic variety in anybody's book.
In almost 30 years of psychic research - never before had I come
across such a large repertoire of phenomena connected with any
physical medium past or present."

It already sounds very bizarre!

Hold on - it's now time to really dig into Scole's evidence, and in order to
do so I can see no better way than telling you the story of the investigation
that the SPR carried out and of the explosive *Scole Report* produced by the
SPR investigators.

So, the SPR validated the phenomena?

Be patient for a minute, will you? The investigation was undertaken by the
SPR several months after reports of the extraordinary happenings in Scole
began circulating in the psychic press. Extraordinary happenings, in the
Society's view, required extraordinary scrutiny and so they decided to
deploy three of the highest calibers at their disposal.

The investigators' team was composed of Montague Keen – whom we
have already encountered a few days ago -, Arthur Ellison, Professor
Emeritus of Electrical and Electronic Engineering at City University,
London, and professor David Fontana, whom we also already met before.

The three investigators have between them more than a century of interest and research into psychic phenomena.

And?

And, let's first look at the main points of what the *Scole Report* has to say about the investigation in general:

Duration. Two years, with monthly 2-3 hour sittings (37 in total) with the Scole Group plus additional sittings as detailed below.

Setting. Venue: A cellar in the Foys' house converted into dedicated séance room. Construction: brick walls, floors and ceiling. Accessible only by a single staircase with a lockable door at the top. Available for thorough search by the investigators both before and after all sittings.

Furniture: round table (approx. 1.2m diameter), obstructed underneath to prevent clandestine movement; upright plastic stacking chairs; trolley holding audio tape recorder. All sittings at Scole were held around this table.

Additional Sittings Additional sittings were held in the home of Dr. Hans Schaer in Zurich (Switzerland), in Dr. Schaer's holiday retreat on the Mediterranean island of Ibiza, in two venues in the USA, and in other European locations. Phenomena were variable across locations, but remained largely consistent with that witnessed at Scole. Dr. Hans Schaer and Montague Keen were present as investigators at the majority of these additional sittings.

Experimental Conditions. The Scole Group, allegedly on the instructions of their 'Spirit Team', agreed to some of the controls requested by the investigators, but could not agree to them all. The Report provides details, and given the fact that sittings were held primarily in darkness, records particular regret at the embargo placed by the 'Spirit Team' upon infra-red and image-intensifying equipment (allegedly because such devices would distract the attention of the investigators, thus disrupting the focused attention said to be necessary for success). However, in the author's opinion sufficient controls operated to render fraud extremely difficult, if not impossible. At no time during the sittings was any direct evidence of fraud apparent to the investigators or to any of their co-investigators.

The 'Spirit Team' maintained that they would 'bring their own light', thus rendering infra-red and image-intensifying equipment redundant, and that they were also working towards the eventual production of phenomena in natural light. The first of these promises was fulfilled to the extent that many of the 'spirit lights' referred to in due course below were sufficiently bright and sustained to allow viewing of the séance room, and the second of them to the extent that Dr. Shaer's final sitting was held in good electric light.

Magician's Testimony. Arguments against fraud were strengthened by the presence of a retired professional stage magician (James Webster, an Associate of the Inner Magic Circle with some 40 years interest in psychical research) at three of the sittings. James Webster testified that in his professional opinion even leading magicians could not duplicate the phenomena he witnessed at Scole without lengthy and expensive preparations, and probably not even then. He further testified that any magician who could produce the Scole effects would rapidly make a fortune on the professional stage.

Right – these seem the same kind of conditions of many other séances we've talked about.

You are indeed correct. Reports written individually by the investigators describe the setting at Scole in much greater details, but the bottom line is the same: room for fraud or trickery was practically non existent.

OK, and now, will we eventually talk phenomena?

Yes. Since, as usual, time is limited, we'll have to look in a succinct way at the phenomena, which were described as "extraordinary in the extreme". To try to combine succinctness and completeness, I'll refer to a presentation made by Professor Fontana at a congress a couple of years ago.

Communications. Different personalities, males and females, each with their own highly distinctive characters, accents and mannerisms, communicated either through the entranced mediums (a male voice could easily come through the female medium, and vice versa) or through direct voices emanating out of thin air in the séance room. Communications amounted to sustained, highly intelligent, witty, informed and technically-precise dialogue, the transcripts of which it is impossible to read without feeling one is eavesdropping on conversation among established friends and professional colleagues. For example, a scientist on the Spirit side would engage Professor Ellison in lengthy discussion on specialist electronics subjects speaking through Alan (a carpenter by trade).

Incidentally, *Spirit voices regularly impressed themselves on a tape recorder from which the microphone had been removed by the investigators.*

The Lights. The light phenomena were among the most dramatic features observed by the investigators. Briefly, the lights consisted chiefly of the following:

- Single light points, varying from the size of peas to that of medium-sized glass marbles, which variously darted around the room at great speed, appeared to pass through the surface of the séance room table (appearing immediately underneath in areas inaccessible to the group), settled on outstretched hands for close inspection, sustained circles in mid-air at a speed and with a precision inconsistent with manual manipulation (often 'switching' off various segments of the circle), responded to requests and apparently entered investigators' bodies, entered crystals placed upon the table and either illuminated the whole crystal or moved as a small point of light throughout their structure, entered a glass dome in the center of the table.

- Small lights which appear to enter, illuminate and levitate crystals.

- Diffused patches of light not reflected off surfaces which traveled around the room at various heights.

- Light sources which took the form of 'materialized' shapes ('robed' figures with brighter patches of light where faces would be) which then floated around the room, touching the investigators on request.

- Lights which illuminated an upturned Pyrex bowl from within, providing sufficient sustained light for 'spirit hands' to be seen by the investigators.

- A light which entered and fully illuminated a crystal in the confines of a Pyrex bowl. The investigators were first invited to touch the illuminated crystal, which turned out to be the solid object that had been initially placed in the bowl. Then, they were asked to take their hands away briefly and then 'feel' the crystal again. *Although still steadily illuminated and apparently unchanged in shape, the crystal on this second investigation offered no resistance to the fingers (i.e. appeared to have become totally insubstantial).* On a third investigation the illuminated crystal was felt once more to be substantial.

- A light which faintly illuminated the inactivated electric light bulb in the center of the room, producing a general glow unconnected with the filament.

- A small light which entered a glass of water held by Professor Fontana and agitated the water, the proximity of the glass to his lips preventing any obvious intrusion of wires or rods.

- A small light which entered and illuminated a table tennis ball which was then projected by unknown forces across the room.

- Lights which illuminated the investigators' feet below the table in areas inaccessible to the group due to the solid foundation upon which the table rested.

- A light which illuminated simultaneously six separate 5-cm solid Perspex supports beneath a glass dome on the table, and which also entered the dome itself.

- A small light which settled on the open palm of a co-investigator (Professor Grattan-Guiness), who then closed his hand to eliminate the possibility of any mechanical attachment to the light.

- A light which built up into a rock-like shape on the table, before levitating, passing in front of one of the investigators (David Fontana) and halting in front of a co-investigator (Ingrid Slack), allowing her to feel its muslin-like texture.

- Diffused patches of light which traveled slowly across the room, appearing to take on the rudimentary shape of human faces with apparent 'lips' that moved in synchronicity with strangled attempts at speech.

The Table. At relatively frequent intervals the table around which the sittings were held commenced a very rapid vibration which could both be heard and felt by the investigators. On occasions, in spite of its solid base, the table then began to swivel round (as evidenced by the movement of luminous tabs placed on the surface at the cardinal points), passing through some 20 degrees before returning to its original position.

<u>Touches</u>. The investigators experienced frequent touches by allegedly spirit hands during the sittings. These touches took the following form:

- A masculine hand associated with a 'direct voice' phenomenon which, at his request, found with immediate accuracy Professor Fontana's hand, grasped and shook it.

- Small, child-like, feminine hands which gently touched and stroked the hands of the investigators.

- Perfectly formed hands apparently ending at the wrist, visible in dark outline by the illumination of attendant 'spirit lights'.

- Touches on the legs of the investigators at points inaccessible to the Scole Group without detection.

- Hands which placed objects in the palms of investigators at request and with unerring accuracy (explicable by normal means only if the Scole Group are credited with infra-red viewers or image intensifiers).

- Hands which grasped those of the investigators' and raised their arms to full extension above their heads.

- Hands which gave playful slaps on the wrist to Montague Keen.

<u>Apports</u>. Several small apports appeared during the investigation, though the Scole Group had a wide range of more impressive objects which had apparently appeared during their closed sittings. One of the most notable of their apports was a copy of the Daily Mail newspaper of 1 April 1944 containing an account of the celebrated trial of medium Helen Duncan. In his article *The Scole Experiment Five Years Later*, Professor Fontana writes:

"The Scole Group received it after being told by one of their communicators that Mrs Duncan would bring them something as evidence of her interest in their work. A natural objection advanced by one of our colleagues to the authenticity of the apport was that the pristine condition of the newspaper indicated it was no more than a modern facsimile reproduction of the original. Accordingly, Montague Keen took the paper to the Print Industries Research Association, a world authority on paper and printing, who informed him in due course that their detailed examination of the typeface demonstrated that it had been printed by letterpress, a long-since obsolete technique. Furthermore, their chemical analysis of the paper on which the apport was printed revealed it to be Second World War newsprint, long since unavailable. In his further investigations, Montague Keen ascertained that the apported version differed from the copy of the Daily Mail for April 1st 1944 kept in the British Library only in that it was an earlier edition of that day's print run.

We therefore have in the apport a tangible piece of evidence (a so-called Permanent Paranormal Object) for which there is no normal explanation. Even if a devout spiritualist had kept a copy of the newspaper back in 1944 as a memento of the legally martyred Helen Duncan, it would hardly have been in pristine condition 60 years later. Even careful vacuum packing and secure sealing against the intrusion of light and air, although it might have helped delay the yellowing of the wartime newsprint, would hardly have maintained it in this condition for such a lengthy period of time. In addition, the notion that someone would have had access to the necessary technology and expertise for doing this back in 1944, with the Second World War still at its height, surely stretches the bounds of credibility to breaking point."

My God. Once again, I'm completely speechless.

And, believe it or not, there's more to come! Tomorrow we will look in some detail at "the films", probably the most incredible phenomenon witnessed by the investigators. We'll also touch upon the séances held by the Group in other countries and, given my own passion in that field, talk about music.

Day 17 - Pictures and music at Scole

Yesterday you were mentioning "the films". Are we talking movies?

Well... yes and no! There was in fact something produced through a video camera, but the extraordinary evidence – in terms of quantity *and* quality - I want to tell you about comes from photographic films.

Stills? Have they taken pictures of ghosts?

No, those whom you call "ghosts" produced images on unexposed color films.

Interesting. What kind of images?

I'll show you in a wee while. Just let me dwell for a minute on the procedural aspects, as their analysis will enormously add to the weight of the evidence. You know, we are talking about the possible production of "PPOs", or Permanent Paranormal Objects, the most elusive and challenging product of psychic research... You will understand that the SPR investigators put extraordinary effort into making sure that the possibility for fraud was minimized. So minimized, in fact, that I personally feel comfortable that we are really looking at PPOs. As usual, though, I'll let you make your own decisions.

Good. Tell me.

OK – first and foremost, all images were produced on brand new, factory sealed films. In most experiments, the films were actually purchased by the investigators themselves and never left their possession during the séance. Typically, the investigators would also secretly mark the carton box containing the film, so to make absolutely sure that the film they had at the end of the experiment was the same they had in the beginning. At the end of the séance, after having satisfied themselves that they were dealing with the same film they themselves had purchased and that the film was in its original, unopened, factory-sealed box, they would proceed themselves to develop it on the premises. In certain experiments, *the films were developed directly by Polaroid's own laboratory in the UK,* as the company had become interested in the very unusual work carried out at Scole.

Well, that looks serious enough.

No. Not enough. The SPR researchers and the Scole Group really wanted to satisfy even the most stubborn critics, so they carried out several experiments adding one additional precaution: the films were placed in a specially designed container, very difficult to open.

"Very difficult"? But, then, at least in principle it could have been opened and the film tampered with...

Yes, it could, albeit with considerable difficulty. If it were not that, in at least one experiment, *the box was permanently held by one of the researchers!*

Oh. And still, images were produced?

Of course. Let's read the short description of that particular experiment as provided by Montague Keen.

> "Space limiting me to only a sketch of one example here, readers are directed to the appendices of the Report which describe in painstaking detail the procedures adopted for obtaining, on 22 November 1996, the images on the "Wie der Staub in [...] Wind" film. Briefly put, the SPR's associate Dr. Walter Schnittger took complete control of all arrangements for the purchasing, storing, unpacking, making secure (locking up in a specially-made box), unlocking, retrieving, and processing of the film used in that sitting. The film,

still in its sealed inner wrapping, was thus placed in a specially-designed, padlocked box (keys stored off-site) and held by Dr. Schnittger throughout the experiment in a fashion that defied all tampering. Just over three years later, he came from Germany to the Scole Study Day to give an eloquent and concise (under-five-minute) account of the exact design of the box (he is a leading engineer) and the exact way in which he had held it during the experiment: three fingers pressed against one side; his thumb against another; his index finger on the top face; his palm covering the lock; the base resting firmly on the table. Only the side facing away from him (the base excepted) was uncovered by any part of his hand, and this side was slotted into the box from above and could not be removed without first dismantling the box from the top. What emerged from the box was conclusively what went into the box, and this was a new, sealed roll of camera film, which when processed was found to carry some lines of poetry in the style of a known Romantic German poet, preceded by various glyphs, designs, and squiggles."

Gosh!

Yes. And now, let's look at some of the pictures. This first one, received in early 1996 on a factory-sealed 25mm Polaroid slide film, contains Sanskrit verses from the Hindu spiritual classic *Srimad Bhagavatam*.

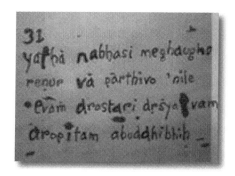

The second one, received on 28 March 1994, contains a somewhat blurred image of the river Seine in Paris, apparently taken from the top of the Notre Dame Cathedral. The third, received on the same day, represents a bearded, turbaned man. The Group thought it might have been Raji, one of the spirit guides from the spirit team, but was later told it was not.

The fourth picture I've selected for you is particularly dramatic. It is the famous picture of London's St Paul's Cathedral taken during the Blitz. When investigators took the bother to check, though, *it appeared that the dimensions of the Cathedral are slightly distorted compared with the original picture.*

And then, let's move from single images to pictures transmitted on entire rolls of color films. The first one was received during a session attended by Professor Archie Roy, whom we encountered in the early days, and transports us back into cross communications. It consists of a phrase in Latin (*Perfectio consummata feu Quinta Essentia Universalis*). The writing was followed by a circle with a dot in the centre. Archie Roy, who, as you may recall, is an astronomy professor, pointed out that this was a symbol for the sun, theories about which had been mentioned in the astronomical discussion he had been having earlier with the spirit team.

Incredibly enough, this symbol was traced back to an image – originally contained in a German publication of 1747 - referring to the 'Golden Chain of Homer'.

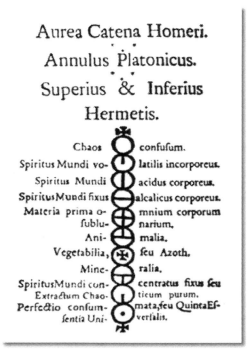

Aurea Catena Homeri.

Annulus Platonicus.

Superius & Inferius

Hermetis.

Chaos	confusum.
Spiritus Mundi vo-	latilis incorporeus.
Spiritus Mundi	acidus corporeus.
Spiritus Mundi fixus	alcalicus corporeus.
Materia prima o-	mnium corporum
fublu-	narium,
Ani-	malia.
Vegetabilia,	feu Azoth.
Mine-	ralia,
Spiritus Mundi con-	centratus fixus feu
Extractum Chao-	ticum purum.
Perfectio confum-	mata, feu Quinta Ef-
fentia Uni-	verfalis.

As you can see, on this chain are attached a number of symbols, one of which has a circle with a dot in the centre and a small cross below. At the base of the image there is the sentence *Pefectio Consummata feu Quinta Essentia Universals*. The Golden Chain symbolises a journey which begins with chaos and confusion, and ends with perfection, thus representing Man's progress towards the Light.

The following image is one meter in length. It contains the phrase "Can you see behind the moon", the meaning of which remains obscure.

Same applies for the glyphs on another one meter long image, which mentions the name of Louis Daguerre, an early pioneer of photography, famous for "Daguerrotypes".

172

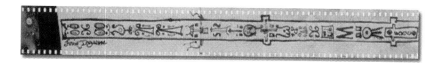

Finally, I want to show you something that I found *really* extraordinary. It's a sketch of the Germanium receptor (which was followed by written instructions in another image) received on 11 January 1997. The electrical diagram was to help Professor Ellison assist the group in building the receptor that would enable verbal communication between the Scole group and the spirit team. Spirit voices were first heard through this device ten days after the image was received.

There, again – I must admit that the evidence is bewildering. Could it not be that the mediums – or somebody in the Scole Group – had particularly developed psychokinetic abilities?

I'm sorry – no. As we have seen in the early days, PK effects are very real but also very tiny: they only show up using particularly sensitive methodologies. To date there is no laboratory evidence that individuals are capable of producing anything even remotely approaching the macro PK effects witnessed at Scole. And then, reflect - anybody capable of producing these effects through their own abilities would rapidly become psychic superstars and go on to earn fame and wealth!

You told me that the group held sessions in other places than the 'Scole hole'.

Yes, indeed. Sessions were organized not only in different places, but even in different countries!

And the same phenomena were produced?

Exactly. Particularly interesting was the time when the Scole team traveled to California and demonstrated their results in nine separate sessions. One was a "scientists session" for NASA physicists and engineers and representatives of Stanford University. The Scole team did not know who was going to attend or where the session would be held, and before the demonstration began the scientists searched the room, a basement gymnasium. A Native American materialized during the session, dancing and chanting, and drums which were mounted high on the wall began to beat. Then familiar spirits appeared, calling some of the scientists by name though their identities were unknown to the Scole team, and explained to the group that the area was an ancient sacred site, and the peoples who had lived there long ago were influencing the session. Most interestingly, some of the American scientists later started a group of their own.

Now – you wanted to talk to me about music. What other incredible story do you have?

It's a particularly touching episode involving Montague Keen. I'll let him tell you about that directly, and then I'll tell you about the amazing results of the research that was carried out at a later stage.

> "Professor Fontana was holding the Panasonic tape recorder containing his carefully marked blank tape. Professor Ellison had duly checked to ensure that there was no microphone in it. We knew the aim was to try to record something paranormal on this tape, but without reproducing any of our own or the spirit voices.
>
> We were told it was to be music; then (in tones of delight) that the composer himself was to transmit it. After a few minutes, clearly heard through much white noise, as though coming from an infinite distance, were sounds which I soon recognised as one of the first pieces of classical music I knew and loved as a boy. It had always had a uniquely strong association with an emotionally stressful period of my youth. The taped record of what was heard at that sitting (as distinct from the tape which David was holding) is eloquent testimony to my startled reaction and profound emotion.
>
> How could 'they' possibly have known? Marvellous enough to produce what is popularly if erroneously called Electronic Voice Phenomena (EVP) on tape; but to have produced a substantial chunk of Rachmaninoff's second piano concerto, orchestra and all, from the discarnate mind (whence else?) clearly meant that 'they' must somehow have divined my buried memories."

That's indeed a lovely story! But you said research...

Yes. Let's hear what Prof. Fontana had to say in an article in which he looked at the Scole experiment five years later and considered new pieces of evidence that had appeared since the original experiments.

"The first is the identification by Guy Playfair of an anomaly in the recording of the Rachmaninov 2nd Piano Concerto which we received - on an audio tape supplied and secretly marked by ourselves - apparently by paranormal means at Scole. The incident is fully described on pages 297-300 of the Scole Report, and we were told by the communicators that the composer was `going to play it himself ... as a projected memory'. We were also told that the music was a gift to one of us (Montague Keen) as a special treat, and Mr. Keen, who was deeply moved by the music, confirmed subsequently that it had been a mainstay of his inner life during a lonely period of his childhood, a fact he had never divulged to his fellow investigators or to the Scole Group.

The controls operating when the music was received are described in the Report, but the anomaly identified by Guy Playfair is unlikely to be identified by anyone without his familiarity with the piece concerned. *It is the erroneous repetition of a cadenza, an error that is unlikely in the extreme to occur in any recording of the piece.* Taken together with the controls operating at the time and the fact that the music was announced in advance by the communicators, this rules out the notion that the music was the result of a stray radio transmission captured by chance by the audio tape recorder."

Day 18 - Electronic Voice Phenomena

All that I have heard and read forces me to believe that the voices come from transcendental, individual entities. Whether it suits me or not, I have no right to doubt the reality of the voices.
Prof. Gebhard Frei, Jung Institute

I think I know what you're going to talk about today.

Do you?

Yes, and, funnily enough, after all we've been discussing over the last couple of weeks, our subject today brought back a very distant memory.

Tell me.

It's not really a story – just a flash, a passing image from almost 40 years ago...

You were in primary school then.

I was in sixth grade. I clearly remember one of my schoolmates telling the story of somebody else leaving a tape recorder in the recording position in an empty room, and then coming back and finding voices recorded on tape. I don't remember the person, but I clearly remember the setting, the classroom, and the fact that at the time I considered the

thing of little interest. I remembered it for all those years, though...

Oh, very good! This is indeed one of the so-called Electronic Voice Phenomena. This, what you're telling me, would have taken place in the mid-sixties, wouldn't it?

No, this would have been 1971. Why?

Because there was hardly any talk of EVP back then. In fact, one of the first pieces of evidence appeared just a couple of decades earlier and was kept confidential until the 1990's. Let me tell you the story, as it is very interesting and also touches upon the involvement of the Catholic Church in the debate on Spirit communication.

This particular episode happened in 1952, and involved two Catholic priests of very high stature. Father Ernetti was a physicist, and Father Agostino Gemelli was the founder of the Catholic University of Milan and President of the Papal Academy. Both men were also world renowned scholars in the rarefied field of "archaic music", classical music dating from before the 10th century. One day, 15 September to be precise, they were having one of the their treasured moments together as they were attempting to transfer a rare and very old performance of Gregorian chant from the wire where it had been originally recorded to a tape recorder. Problem was that the old wire kept breaking and at some stage they started feeling they were going nowhere with their work.

In a moment of exasperation, Father Gemelli called out to his deceased father for help, as he would do on such occasions. The story says that things remained quite difficult on the technical side but, to the complete amazement of the two priests, when they played back the tape they could clearly hear the voice of Father Gemelli's father saying "Of course I shall help you. I'm always with you."

The experiment was repeated, and this second experiment produced a very clear voice filled with humour saying, "But Zuccone, it is clear, don't you know it is I?"

'Zuccone' is an Italian expression used to lovingly address a child who doesn't (or doesn't want to) understand something. Such an expression was apparently typical of Father Gemelli's father.

During the following weeks, Father Gemelli was reportedly torn between feelings of joy for this apparent proof of survival and the fear of contravening the teachings of his own Church in entertaining communication with the dead. The matter had to be settled, however, and, owing to their stature and to the exceptional nature of the events, the two men were granted a private audience with Pope Pius XII in Rome. Once the deeply troubled Father Gemelli had explained his experience, much to his surprise the Pope reassured him by saying "Dear Father Gemelli, you really need not worry about this. The existence of this voice is strictly a scientific fact and has nothing whatsoever to do with spiritism. The recorder is totally objective. It receives and records only sound waves from wherever they come. This experiment may perhaps become the cornerstone for a building for scientific studies which will strengthen people's faith in a hereafter." Despite this reassurance, however, Father Gemelli made sure that the experiment did not go public until the last years of his life, with the results finally published only in 1990.

Very intriguing, as usual!

Isn't it? But hold on - let me briefly recap what I've learned on the position of the Church with respect to such communications. For the last sixty years, it appears that the Catholic Church has crossed paths with EVP research on several occasions, mostly at a very senior level. The reverend Gabhard Frei I quoted to you in the beginning, for example, was not only an internationally recognized parapsychologist and the co-founder of the Jung Institute, but Pope Pius XII's own cousin. Incidentally, Professor Frei died on 27 October 1967. In November 1967 at numerous taping sessions a voice giving its name as Gebhard Frei came through. The voice was identified by Prof. Peter Hohenwarter of the University of Vienna as positively belonging to Dr Frei.

Ha!

Also, it is very interesting to learn that Pope Paul VI was well aware of the work being done from 1959 onwards on the voice phenomena by one of the giants in this field, the Swede Friedrich Jurgenson. How come? Simple – before and on top of being one of the founding fathers of EVP research, Jurgenson was a film producer and had made a documentary film about the Pope. In a letter to a fellow researcher, Jurgenson – whose work we'll discuss later – wrote: "I have found a sympathetic ear for the Voice Phenomenon in the Vatican." Paul VI made Jurgenson a Knight Commander of the Order of Saint Gregory the Great in 1969.

The Vatican also apparently gave permission for its own priests to conduct their own research. Father Leo Schmid in Switzerland collected thousands of voices and published an account of his research in his 1976 book *When the Dead Speak*. Another researcher was Father Andreas Resch who, after conducting his own experiments began courses in parapsychology at the Vatican's school for priests in Rome. In 1970 the International Society for Catholic Parapsychologists held a conference in Austria and a major part of that conference was concerned with papers on the Electronic Voice Phenomena. In England in 1972 four senior members of the Catholic Church were involved in the famous Pye recording studio tests, which I'll describe to you in due course. The position of the Church was finally made official in 1995 through an article on the Vatican's newspaper *Osservatore Romano*. There you can read: "According to the modern catechism, God allows our dear departed persons who live in an ultra-terrestrial dimension to send messages to guide us in certain difficult moments of our lives. The Church has decided not to forbid any more the dialogue with the deceased with the condition that these contacts are carried out with a serious religious and scientific purpose."

I can't help thinking about the "many sticks" theory.

Why just now?

I don't know… It strikes me again. All these hundreds, thousands of people you keep telling me about - can they all be fools, misguided, naïve, fraudsters? And all this truly colossal mass of evidence from the most diverse and unrelated fields – can it be just one gigantic, coordinated deception? The biggest farce in human history?

Aw, right. A moment of insight. I know those! I better let you reflect on that for a moment.

Now, let me tell you a few more stories. Among the mass of information available, I'll focus on the work of some individuals and on some events of particular significance. Inevitably, I'll have to begin with the one who's unanimously considered the founding father of EVP research – the very Friedrich Jurgenson I've already mentioned a moment ago.

Jurgenson is really not an easy guy to describe in a few words. He was so full of talents, and achieved so much in his life that a few lines of biography don't do him any justice. This very unusual character was born in Odessa, Ukraine, in 1903. His mother was Swedish and his father was of Danish descent, practicing as a physician in Odessa where the family had moved to from Estonia. Jurgenson trained as a painter at the Art Academy and as a singer and musician at the Odessa Conservatory. Before World War II, he lived in Estonia, Palestine and Italy, continuing his training and started making a living as a classical singer and painter. During the war, he moved to Stockholm, where he married and became a Swedish citizen. He progressively abandoned singing as he was getting increasingly in demand as a painter, specializing in portraits and in the reproduction of archaeological works. His work on Pompeii and on the relics buried under the Vatican brought him to the attention of Pope Pius XII, who commissioned several portraits from him.

His accidental discovery of EVP was made on June 12, 1959, when he and his wife Monica went to visit their country house to enjoy the warm summer. Jurgenson brought his tape-recorder to record the singing of wild birds, especially the chaffinch. Listening to the tape he:

> "…heard a noise, vibrating like a storm, where you could only remotely hear the chirping of the birds. My first thought was that maybe some of the tubes had been damaged. In spite of this I switched on the machine again and let the tape roll. Again I heard this peculiar noise and the distant chirping. Then I heard a trumpet solo, a kind of a signal for attention. Stunned, I continued to listen when suddenly a man's voice began to speak in Norwegian. Even though the voice was quite low I could clearly hear and understand the words. The man spoke about 'nightly bird voices' and I perceived a row of piping, splashing and rattling sounds. Suddenly the choir of birds and the vibrating noise stopped. In the next moment the chirping of a chaffinch was heard and you could hear the tits singing at a distance - the machine worked perfectly!"

From there onwards, Jurgenson continued to investigate these phenomena and at first he thought the voices were somehow coming from extraterrestrial intelligences. Then, he was to experience an event that would change his life:

"I was outside with a tape recorder, recording bird songs. When I listen through the tape, a voice was heard to say 'Friedel, can you hear me. It's mammy...' It was my dead mothers voice. 'Friedel' was her special nickname for me."

Jurgenson then decided to go public with his discoveries. He wrote a book, published in 1964, and called a press conference to launch it. As one would expect, he attracted considerable interest, and considerable skepticism. Interest, however, also came from reputable research institutions, such as the Max Plank Institute, the University of Freiburg and the US Parapsychological Association. And, what is most important, other researchers came, learned, and started their own work with tape recorders: EVP research was officially born and would deliver an extraordinary quantity of evidence over the coming decades.

Jurgenson himself continued his own research until his death in 1987. Meanwhile, he also became a producer of documentary films for the Swedish National TV, including the one on the life of Pope Paul VI that we mentioned earlier. He published two more books on the subject of EVP and held hundreds of lectures. In 2000, the Friedrich Jurgenson Foundation was set up to preserve his work as an EVP researcher and as an artist.

Did anybody continue Jurgenson's research work?

More than continue – in fact we could almost say that the next character we'll encounter "stole" the research from Jurgenson, as for many years EVP has been referred to as "Raudive voices".

Raudive?

Yes - that is Dr. Konstantin Raudive. This pioneer of EVP reserach was born in Latvia and later became a student of Carl Jung. He then went on to be a psychologist and a psychology professor at the University of Uppsala in Sweden. He studied parapsychology all his life, and, after being exposed to the work of Friedrich Jurgenson, he himself became very interested in the survival hypothesis. It was in 1964 that Raudive read Jürgenson's book, *Voices from Space*, and was so impressed by it that he arranged to meet Jürgenson in 1965.

He then worked with Jürgenson (you can see both of them with their equipment in the picture) to make some EVP recordings, but their first efforts bore little fruit. In the beginning all they could hear were very weak, muddled voices. Things were to change abruptly shortly after, however, as one night, as he listened to one recording, he clearly heard a number of voices. When he played the tape over and over, he came to understand all of them, some of which were in German, some in Latvian, some in French. The last voice on the tape, a woman's voice, said "Va dormir, Margarete" ("Go to sleep, Margaret"). Raudive later wrote: "These words made a deep impression on me, as Margarete Petrautzki had died recently, and her illness and death had greatly affected me."

Raudive started researching such voices on his own and spent much of the last ten years of his life exploring EVP. With the help of various electronics experts he recorded over 100,000 snippets on audiotapes, most of which under what he described as "strict laboratory conditions." Over 400 people were involved in his research, and all apparently heard the voices. This culminated in the 1968 publication of *Unhörbares wird hörbar* (published in English in 1971 as *Breakthrough*).

In 2002, the National Sound Archive (NSA) of the British Library acquired a number of the original Raudive tapes. On the NSA official bulletin, Toby Oakes comments:

> "There is no doubt that the recordings evince a curious phenomenon. Inexplicable, voice-like sounds can be discerned on recordings made under stringent experimental conditions (sound engineers at the Pye laboratories pronounced themselves baffled after one such exercise sponsored by the Sunday Mirror in 1971)."

The "Pye laboratories" Mr. Oakes refers to are in fact the ultra-famous Pye recording studios in London, UK. The 1971 experiments were carried out in the studios, so that not only any external sound source could be effectively filtered out, but – and even more importantly – the technicians of Pye could ascertain that the equipment used was of top quality and had not been tampered with. After some 200 voices were recorded in the space of 27 minutes (*and none of them was heard until playback*), Ken Attwood, Chief Engineer of Pye, stated:

> "I have done everything in my power to break the mystery of the voices without success; the same applies to other experts. I suppose we must learn to accept them."

I'm not even surprised any more...

I know... Now, instead of continuing to tell you individual EVP stories – believe me, we could be here for a long time! – I would like to go technical a little bit, and discuss some of the features of the voices that have so frequently been recorded during the last 70 years. To do so, I will refer to the work of Dr. Ernst Senkowski, a physics professor and former military communication specialist from Mainz, Germany, who coined the term Instrumental Trans Communication (ITC), which is the subject we'll explore tomorrow.

Prof. Senkowski was an active EVP experimenter on his own, but never claimed to have reached extraordinary results in the production of paranormal voices. Instead, he participated in and closely observed the work of other researchers, studying their methodologies and – especially – their results, and is probably the only one to have published scientific papers on the subject. A very interesting summary of his work can be found in the paper *Analysis of Anomalous Audio and Video Recordings*, presented before the US Society for Scientific Exploration in June 1995.

The first thing that Senkowski did was to come up with a simple "cutoff" criterion to separate meaningful results from non meaningful ones. An audio signal, he reminds us, never exists in isolation – it is always accompanied by noise (the hiss of a tape recorder, the static crashes of a radio, the ambient noise in even the quietest of rooms). In the case of EVP recordings, if what is called signal to noise ratio (S/N) is less than 1, the signal is buried in noise and the recording lends itself to fantasies, hallucinations and therefore incorrect interpretation due to wishful thinking. The same can be said for recordings in which S/N is approximately 1: here the signal is about as strong as the noise, and, according to Senkowski, the material is not yet good enough for accurate scientific study. Only recordings with a S/N larger than 1 are worth investigating – they lend themselves to correct interpretation by the listeners and can be the subject of scientific analysis.

The second thing Senkowski tells us is that recordings with a good S/N are extremely rare.

Extremely rare?

Yes. You may remember that the very first day of our conversation I told you about the masses of responses you get if you Google "electronic voice phenomena".

Vaguely.

Well, I was using that example to point at the difference between the masses of dubious (and, in most cases, outright laughable) "evidence" and the relatively very few but stunning cases of good evidence. The case of EVP is particularly well suited, because the technology is simple and anybody with a tape recorder thinks they can reproduce the experiments. And, when they get noise on tape, think they hear things that nobody else can hear.

Aren't you being a bit hard?

Listen to yourself! Were you not the skeptical one? Really – do listen to some of these examples on the Internet and you'll understand what I'm saying.

But, then, what are the good ones like?

Exactly. This is the main reason why I brought Senkowski's research into the discussion. From his studies, we learn that true EVP are distinctive: they have a distinctive character of cadence, pitch, frequency, volume and use of background sound. The voices have a distinctive sound to them that is difficult to describe. For instance, EVP messages often have an unusual speed of enunciation; the words seem to be spoken more quickly than normal human speech. The best way I can describe it is that it's almost as if each word is spoken quickly, yet the pauses between the words are of a natural length. The combination of these two speed factors makes for the peculiar rhythm and perceived speed. You may also notice that the paranormal voices often have a hollow and/or monotone quality. Plus, the enunciation of words is not just faster, but the frequency range of the phrases is sometimes higher than normal human speech.

Italian researcher Paolo Presi at the University of Turin has reported that spectral analysis of EVP samples shows that the fundamental frequencies of voice associated with the human voice box are sometimes missing in EVP. He describes the typical EVP as a "thickening" of the background noise to form the voice. Furthermore, sounds are often heard prior to an occurrence of EVP. Although these vary in nature, they tend to be within tenths of a second of a phrase and are "popping" or "clicking" noises.
Secondly, EVP show evidence of being limited by available energy. In Scotland, Alexander MacRae has noted that the utterances tend to have about the same amount of audio power in their associated sound wave from one EVP sample to another.

What?

Yes, it's not difficult to understand: it means that a short EVP will tend to be louder than a long EVP. A long phrase might therefore be composed of two or more shorter phrases separated by minor pauses. Also, an utterance may trail off at the end, as if the energy is being depleted before the message is delivered. This is as if the communicator is attempting to manage available power as "packets" of energy. The evidence is very strong that EVP are energy-limited phenomena.

Oh...

This is a curious phenomenon, and it has been studied in depth by several researchers. For instance, another Italian, Dr. Carlo Trajna, analyzed some 24,000 snippets of EVP and plotted the relative frequency distribution of the words based on their length measured in number of syllables. His plots show a well marked peak around 5 syllables. These results were independently confirmed by Senkowski, using EVP recordings from experimenters different from the ones used by Trajna.

Another independent confirmation came from McRae, who, by the way, is a former NASA communications specialist, who determined peaks around 1,6 sec/recording, in good agreement with 5 syllables. McRae considered this "time-packaging" a clear sign of the improbability of such passages and experimentally rejected the hypothesis that complete structures of this kind could result as stochastic (that is, purely random) cut-outs from normal sentences.

Once more - what?

This proves that EVP are *not* stray pieces from normal radio broadcasts or two-way communications.

All right.

To describe the fact that the voices prefer short words with few syllables, Trajna invented the term "Psychophonic Style". He compared 24,000 words taken from normal writings of four authors with the 24,000 words we mentioned before. His findings are very interesting: first of all, the psychophonic style words are on average 20% shorter (as number of syllables) than the words from the authors (this is a value that was confirmed independently by Senkowski). Secondly, Trajna found out that the differences among the words of the four authors were *greater* than those among the psychophonic recordings. Finally, the effects are apparently independent of the language of the recorded utterances (they were at least observed in Italian, German and English). What does this tell you?

That the psychphonic style is a coherent, unique style, different from common language and independent from the language used.

Fantastic! Completely correct. Finally, something that I found extremely interesting is the relationship between the experimenter and the results of the experiments. Research shows that the experimenter's excitement in trying a new detection device or recording technique may be the source of improved EVP collection. As the new approach becomes "normal operating procedure," the improvements generally fade back to more average results. This suggests that it is important for the experimenter to maintain a keen personal interest during experiments. This is also one of the reasons it is put forward that the experimenter is an integral part of the recording circuit. The experimenter is apparently supplying the necessary psi energy to enable a nonphysical to physical transfer of energy.

In the same vein, we must note that exceptionally effective EVP and – as we will see tomorrow – ITC collecting systems have been developed. However, these typically work well for the developer, but do not work as well for other experimenters. This evidence supports the hypothesis that the experimenter is part of the recording circuit. It has also reinforced the concept that the communicating entity may be specific to the experimenter. The existence of operator-dependent signatures in weak-psychokinesis experiments and the comparison of their results with different systems suggested that *individual faculties are the primary variables in the experiments,* whereas the special type of the technical device is less important. That agrees with Senkowski's experiences: low level results are obtained by practically everybody with enough motivation and patience, whereas peak results like high quality direct voices or clear images on TV-screens are achieved by operators who are specially gifted – say strongly psychic.

Day 19 - Instrumental Trans-Communication

"I tell you, dear listeners of Radio Luxembourg, and I swear by the life of my children, that nothing has been manipulated. There are no tricks. It is a voice, and we do not know from where it comes."

What is this now?

This, when you hear the original recording, is quite a dramatic quote. That's the broken, distraught voice of radio presenter Rainer Holbe, during a broadcast on the evening of January 15, 1982.

What happened?

Well, this is yet another gem. It's one of the hundreds of incredible stories that I came across in my studies, and I think it's a good introduction for today's subject. The story – or at least the part of the story the quote refers to – is quite simple, actually. It's about a German electronics engineer, Hans-Otto Koenig, who, studying the work of other pioneers of the sector, had put together a relatively sophisticated device with which he claimed he could entertain two-way communications with the deceased.

So, this is what instrumental trans-communication is all about?

Yes, indeed. Whilst EVP are mostly about one way-communication (although, in fact, some of the voices recorded on tape did actually answer questions asked by the experimenters), ITC is about coherent, sustained and real-time communication between the two sides. Isn't that incredible in itself? I mean, just the idea…

Incredible it is, for sure. But then, again, what happened in January 1982?

Ah, yes, of course. That night, Koenig had been invited to demonstrate his "Koenig's generator" during a live broadcast of the now defunct Radio Luxemburg, once the most popular shortwave radio station in Europe. During the afternoon, the equipment had been set up in one of the studios under the watchful eye of the Radio Luxembourg engineers. Then, as the live show got underway, the "generator" was connected to a set of speakers and switched on. An engineer asked if voices would come through on request. Within seconds, a clear voice was heard. It said quite simply: *"Otto Koenig makes wireless with the dead".* Understandably pandemonium broke out. Another question was asked and seconds later a voice replied: *"We hear your voice".* That was when Rainer Holbe, the show's host and quite a celebrity at the time, broke into the live transmission with his now famous quote. A week or so later, Radio Luxembourg published an official *communiqué* in which it confirmed that the program had been strictly supervised, and the staff and engineers were convinced that the voices heard during the program were paranormal.

Aw – again, that's fantastic stuff!

I know, I know. I must admit, though, that, at these final stages of our conversations, I am really tired, worn out.

How so?

Well, I think it's because of the extraordinary – for me – effort of having to select the stories to tell you among the sea of evidence I have frequently spoken to you about. It's a pain – honestly. I would like to tell you everything I've read, all the stories, all the incredible cases. Every story seems to me especially meaningful, particularly intriguing, something that cannot be left out. But that's obviously impossible: we don't have the time, and I, probably, wouldn't have the energy. So I have to ponder over the decisions of what to focus on – just the few cases that will help me in conveying the overwhelming impression of collective proof that I myself feel.

But you've done that already. It'll take me a very long time to elaborate all we've been discussing, to try to make some sense of it, but I honestly feel that I've seen enough white flies to give up on my conviction that only black flies exist.

I appreciate you saying that. I very much like the idea of having presented enough evidence to at least make you consider the position of the survivalists. Still, in the particular case of ITC, I would have at the very least a dozen different stories, each supported by extraordinary evidence and it pains me to have to choose…

Ach, come on! Just keep the enthusiasm going! Tell me a couple of good stories, and perhaps I'll research the other ones myself.

OK, then, I'll stick to two. One is a story from the US, and the other one from Italy. You may want to note, by the way, that most of the research on ITC was not carried out in the Anglo-Saxon world, and that therefore much of the interesting literature on the subject is in German, Spanish, Italian and Portuguese. So, let's start with George Meek, his *Spiricom*, and another extraordinary tale of scientific collaboration with entities on the other side.

Meek was an engineer by training and an inventor by nature. A successful inventor, in fact, to the point that over the years he managed to build a very healthy business in the air conditioning sector, a business from which he retired in 1970, at the age of 60, to devote the rest of his life to psychic research. The peculiar focus of his psychic work was to do exactly what happened independently in Scole over a decade later: to use mediums to contact scientists on the spirit side who would help him build equipment that would have permitted communication between the two worlds. To do so, Meek, who had sold his business and retired a very wealthy man, launched an ambitious program of investigation involving many medical doctors, psychologists, psychiatrists and other scientists in a number of countries in the world.

He and his research teams carried out a wide range of interviews with mediums and healers worldwide. A side-product of his research was a book he co-authored with 14 other researchers of his group (*Healers and the Healing Process*), which is currently recommended by the World Health Organization for health professionals in developing countries. Meanwhile, in the US, he set up a laboratory (which would later be called the Metascience Laboratory), where a team of technicians started experimenting with electronic equipment with the aim of improving the reception of EVP.

Initial results at Metascience were mildly encouraging, but the real breakthrough was to come in 1973, when Meek started collaborating with the American medium William O'Neil. O'Neil said to Meek that he had been contacted by a deceased scientist, one Dr. George Mueller, who was keen on initiating the kind of collaboration Meek was looking for. A fascinating story within the story is the research Meek and his collaborators undertook to ascertain whether Dr. Mueller really had existed and, once it became clear that he really did, to make sure that the mass of details about his life that were being communicated by O'Neil were neither the medium's invention nor accessible in the public domain. Forget names, dates, addresses - all the personal and family data that were researched and found correct. The in-depth investigation concerned, for instance, Mueller's membership of the Haresfoot Club and of the Triangle Fraternity at Wisconsin University, which was confirmed by Professor Norman Uphoff of Cornell University after he discovered old photographs (over thirty years had passed since Mueller's membership of these undergraduate societies, for which written records were not available). Another example concerns the details of a booklet Mueller had written in 1947 for the US Army, *Introduction to Electronics*, of which the Library of Congress had no records and the existence of which was only confirmed after a two-year search of the Wisconsin State Historical Society archives.
Meek therefore satisfied himself that the entity communicating through O'Neil was indeed the disincarnate personality of Dr. George Mueller, a PhD in experimental physics from Cornell University, for which he worked as research fellow before moving to design and development work for the US Signals Corp and for the NASA Space Program at Cape Canaveral.

Under instructions by Mueller, the Metascience technicians built a device which would later be named Spiricom. The principle was to use an acoustic generator to produce 13 of the fundamental frequencies that participate in forming an adult male voice, and to use these audio tones to modulate the radio frequency carrier produced by a common two-way radio. The signal produced by the low-power transmitter was then picked up by a receiver, whose audio output was available for the operator through a loudspeaker. Whatever came out of the loudspeaker was also recorded onto tape for further research. The idea behind the Spiricom was to use discrete audio tones instead of random white noise in order to facilitate the production of paranormal voices, and to provide at least two mechanisms through which spirit communicators could intervene to produce the end results (one at the radio frequency stage, between transmitter and receiver, and one at the audio frequency stage, where sounds are produced by the speaker at the end of the chain).

The results obtained with the Spiricom during the early 1980s were quite stunning. In countless recordings, Mueller can be heard conversing with O'Neil, in a clear but somewhat robotic voice. I have heard some of the recordings, and I immediately thought of the buzzing voice produced through vibrators by people who can't speak normally following tracheotomy. In one of the recordings, Mueller can be heard reciting the nursery rhyme *Mary had a Little Lamb*, then asking O'Neil to play the tape back for him and giving instructions on how to improve the sound.

Meek had the tapes analyzed by the University of Tokyo, which confirmed that Mueller's recorded voice was neither Meek's nor O'Neil's. The Japanese scientists did not rule out that the voices could have been computer-generated, but insisted that such results could only have been possible through the use of technology far beyond Meek's financial means. Again, having heard some of the recordings, I can tell you that the voice sounds completely different from the computer-generated voices I have heard in much more recent times, produced with incomparably more sophisticated equipment. Furthermore, Scottish researcher Alexander McRae, an expert who has worked for NASA on the problem of unscrambling the distorted speech of astronauts and divers when working in a helium-oxygen environment, also concluded in favor of the paranormality of the voices.

What happened then?

Science journalist J. G. Fueller, who provides plenty of details on Meek's experiments in his book *The Ghost of 29 Megacycles*, tells us that Meek was acutely aware of the fact that the results obtained by the Spiricom were largely dependent on O'Neil's mediumistic capabilities. He could not understand to what extent the process was successful because of the electronic device, and was anyway not able to obtain results without the presence of O'Neil. Furthermore, Mueller himself, in his communications, often stressed that he would not be around forever. In fact, from the second half of 1981, Mueller began to make repeated references to the fact that he was "beginning to shed his dense earthly vibrations and was starting his progression upwards" through the various levels of consciousness that are said to exist in the spirit world. Communications through Spiricom became increasingly difficult, and Mueller began giving instructions for the construction of a more sophisticated version of the device, that should have enabled him to continue to communicate.

However, before the construction of the new model could be started, the old Spiricom fell silent.

That was a disappointment.

It was indeed. Meek wanted to have an instrument to communicate with the other side independently from mediums, and clearly failed. At the same time, he could not understand why other spirit communicators would not come through. These questions remained unanswered, but Meek's pioneering work inspired an entire generation of researchers – including the very Hans-Otto Koenig we spoke about in the beginning – who went far beyond the Spiricom results. Some, especially Portuguese researcher Anabela Cardoso, have been able in recent years to demonstrate results independent of the presence of any particular individual. As to variety of communicators… well, it's time to move to the last piece of evidence I'll talk to you about.

After many stories from my country of adoption, Scotland, it's finally the turn of my country of birth, Italy. We'll ideally visit wonderful Tuscany, and meet one of the true icons of ITC, Marcello Bacci. Marcello is a simple man, making a living from a radio and TV repair shop, who has attracted both the attention of the world's foremost psychic researchers and, what is most important, enormous love and gratitude on the part of the hundreds of bereaved families he has helped during the last four decades. Marcello Bacci's specialty, within the broader field of ITC, is technically known as Direct Radio Voices, that is the method that seeks to obtain anomalous communications directly through the loudspeakers of radios, and such voices frequently refer to listeners by name, respond to questions put to them, and sometimes provide relevant and lengthy items of information. For this purpose he favours a valve radio, tuned to white noise in the short-wave band, rather than solid-state technology.

Bacci, who has been consistently successful in obtaining these communications in his own experiments, is principally dedicated to working with bereaved parents, but he is also eager to co-operate with scientists in order to demonstrate the credibility of his results (such as those from Il Laboratorio in Bologna, Italy, the only laboratory in Europe devoted entirely to the scientific testing and analysis of apparently paranormal phenomena). Like all the great people we've encountered in the last weeks, he takes no money for any of this work and does not seek to attract publicity.

Before we move to the core of our last story, I want to tell you something personal. You may remember that, as I was briefly describing myself during our first encounter, I told you that I have a lifelong, active interest in the performing arts.

I don't, but go ahead.

Well, I happen to be a recording and performing musician and producer. Originally a jazz guitarist, I have had the great fortune to be able to turn my passion for music into a professional activity - a parallel career, obviously totally unrelated to my day job as Public Health specialist and university lecturer. Me and my wife, who happens to be a major label recording singer and songwriter, run a small music production company, based in our own recording studio, and as we speak we have some 200,000 CDs around the world with our names on them.

Wow, now – that is really surprising! Congratulations. I wonder how you manage to do all these things... You seem to have an encyclopaedic culture on psychic matters – acquiring that must have taken plenty of your time. Plus, I don't understand why you're telling this to me just now...

Ach, no! I am certainly not a real expert in psychic research! Fair enough, I've read quite a bit, but that doesn't make me a world expert! It's perhaps my work at the university that has taught me to present things effectively, so I may pass for the real expert I am not. And, as far as my engagement with music is concerned, that is important to understand what's behind my own judgment of some particular recordings of Bacci's I happened to listen to.

Oh - music?

Choirs. The most extraordinary, hair-raising polyphonic choirs. Apart fr0m the typical – quite unique, actually – distortion typical of all the ITC voices (regardless of the experimenter, device or recording method used...), what really struck me was the musical character of the recordings. Definitely human voices, resembling Gregorian chant, sacred music, but... different! Different – musically – in a way that's very hard for me to explain. The choice of notes... The way the main melody moves, the way the polyphonic harmonies move beneath it... The style sounds recognizable at first, but then you pay more attention and, no, it's not. A little like somebody had re-written music of ten centuries ago adding some elements of contemporary classical music. But even that is not an appropriate description. After 35 years of studying and making music, my intuition tells me just one thing – *that is not music from this world!*

Gosh, again, I'm amazed...

Hold on, though, let me get to the real story here, and *then* you'll be truly amazed! Let's start by setting the context. The first objection to Bacci's extraordinary Direct Radio Voices would obviously be that he, being a radio technician, arranged a system so that an accomplice would use a transmitter from another room (or a nearby building) to send what appear as paranormal signals when heard through the old valve radio. That would not account for the particular distortion of the radio voices, or the time compression that has been described by all other researchers, and even less for the fact that the radio voices come in many different languages, address people by name, and provide detailed information that proved to hundreds of relatives that they were actually communicating with their deceased children.

To test the "accomplice with secret transmitter" hypothesis, already in 1985 Carlo Trajna, an electronics engineer, set up a second radio right next to that used by Bacci, connected it to the same power lead and to an independent aerial, and tuned to the same short-wave frequency. While Bacci's radio was heard to receive the anomalous voice communications, the second radio was found to be receiving only normal white noise.
From an interesting article in the *ITC Journal* we also learn that:

In a second and equally ground-breaking investigation, Professor Salvatore Festa, professor of Physics at Naples University, and Radio Technician Franco Santi removed the two valves ECC85 (the FM valve) and ECH81 (the AM/SW converter valve) from Bacci's radio during the receipt of anomalous voices, and established that even without these valves (in the absence of which no normal broadcasts can be received in the short wave band), the voices continued unabated. During this experiment Professor Festa also measured the intensities respectively of the electric field and of the magnetic field adjacent to the radio with the radio switched off, and both during normal radio transmission and during the period when the voice phenomenon occurred, and found that these fields did not show any variation when the voices phenomenon started and also that the values measured after the valves were removed but the voices continued were practically identical to the values measured when the radio was turned off. The demonstration that the voices continued even in the absence of the valves and that there was no variation in electric or magnetic fields during their reception provides further convincing evidence that such voices cannot be accounted for by fraudulent transmissions.

In fact, I can see no better way to tell you my last story than to keep referring to the ITC Journal report, describing an experiment that saw the participation – among others – of some of the world-class researchers we've already grown familiar with in previous days. It's a bit long and rich in details. I suggest you consider it with attention – for me, that would be enough evidence in itself...

The present experiment took place in Marcello Bacci's laboratory in Grosseto, Italy, in electric lighting from a blue coloured, wall mounted, 25-watt bulb, situated just above and slightly to the right of the radio and bright enough to allow the investigators to observe closely all movements by Bacci and by each other. Prior to and subsequent to the experiment, the laboratory and the radio used by Bacci were available for full inspection by all those named below. When the experimental sessions commenced, Marcello Bacci seated himself directly in front of his radio, a Normende, Fidelio model, dating from the late 1950s, with Professor Fontana (Professor of Transpersonal Psychology at Liverpool's John Moores University and Chair of the Survival Committee of the Society for Psychical Research) beside him on his left, and Dr. Anabela Cardoso (founder and Editor of the *ITC Journal* and Director of the ITC Journal Research Centre) immediately behind him and positioned so that she could look directly over his left shoulder that she could touch with her chin. Professor Festa, named in connection with one of the two investigations already described, was seated on Dr. Anabela Cardoso's left, and Mr. Robin Foy (leader of the well-known Scole investigation in the UK and an expert in physical psychic phenomena) on Bacci's right. These four investigators were at all times in close touching proximity to Marcello Bacci.

Aeronautical Engineer Paolo Presi (a leading member of Il Laboratorio and a long-standing investigator of the Bacci phenomena) was on Bacci's left, separated from him by Mrs. Laura Pagnotta, daughter of the Mrs. Silvana who has been a close collaborator and observer of Mr. Bacci's work for 20 years, and by Professor Fontana. Radio Technician Franco Santi, named with Professor Festa in connection with the investigation already described, remained free to move around the room for reasons detailed shortly, and Mr. Angelo Toriello and Mr. Sandro Zampieri, both of whom have also been close observers of Mr. Bacci for many years were also in close attendance. In the room there were also a few mothers who had lost their children and other experimenters exceptionally admitted at the session in a total of 37 people.

The radio was situated on a workbench placed against the wall directly facing the investigators, and in a position that made it inaccessible from the rear except by leaning over the bench from the front. There is no back to the radio, and sufficient space was left between it and the wall for radio technician Franco Santi to reach inside by leaning across the bench, as detailed shortly. Inspection prior to the experiment had revealed that there was no access to the radio through apertures in the workbench or in the wall. Behind Bacci and the investigators and separated from them by approximately one and a half metres were rows of chairs on which some of those who attend Bacci's regular sessions for bereaved parents were seated. No member of this latter group took any part in the experiment or approached the radio used by Bacci at any point in the course of it.

Proceedings commenced at 19.10 hours, with Bacci, the investigators and those elsewhere in the room all in their places. Audio tape recorders (analogue and digital) were switched on in order to record proceedings. Bacci began by turning on his radio and selecting the short wave band. He then, as is his usual practice, began slowly to turn the tuning control, scanning the range from 7 to 9 megahertz. As expected, this produced a range of radio transmissions interspersed with white noise. Bacci explained in Italian that he was 'searching for good white noise'. This procedure continued for 15-20 minutes until Bacci pronounced, again in Italian "I can feel them – they will come". At this point he stopped turning the dial, and the white noise was heard to change to a vortex-like sound that could variously be described as wind or the sound of waves.

Shortly afterwards this noise died down (though often it recurred simultaneously with the voices, as if they were in some way 'carried' on its sound) and voices became audible from the radio. The first words were in Italian, and these were followed by words in Spanish. Bacci, again in Italian, informed those responsible for the voices that they could "speak in Portuguese, English or Spanish". The invisible communicators then addressed David Fontana and Robin Foy in English and Anabela Cardoso in Spanish.
In the ensuing session, which lasted in all for approximately one hour, what appeared to be five or six separate voices (one of them possibly female, and the rest male) spoke in English and in Spanish as well as in Italian, some of them with a clarity resembling that of normal voices, others with the sonority that characterises many ITC voices and that renders them distinct from normal articulation. Also present in the voices were the strange semantics that are characteristic of many ITC

communications (e.g. when addressing Dr. Cardoso the communicator referred to her visit to Bacci with the words 'Anabela … you are going to the learning boss'), and the parabolic, wave-like speech rhythms. Sometimes the sound wave carrying the voices became distorted, but in spite of these features the meaning of approximately 70 per cent of the vocal utterances was directly clear to those named above, five of whom are fluent in Italian and English, and one of whom (Dr. Cardoso, a senior Portuguese diplomat by profession who lives in Spain most of the time), is fluent in all the languages used as well as in her mother tongue Portuguese.

The voices referred to those present by their first names, and addressed Professor Fontana by both his first and second names ("David Fontana", perhaps to distinguish him from David Pagnotta, who was present elsewhere in the room), and then added "Ciao David". Bacci himself was frequently referred to either as "Marcello" or as "Bacci". All names were given clearly, and were easily recognisable. Sometimes the voices replied to questions in a different language from that used by the questioner, and sometimes they even changed languages during the course of their answers. Not all questions were answered, and certain of them only after a pause.

The most significant incident during the session, and the one that marks this experiment out as of historic importance in the history not only of ITC research but also of psychical research in general, occurred near the end of the session. As mentioned earlier, the finding by Professor Festa and Technician Santi that removal of two of the valves from the radio did not prevent the receipt of the anomalous voices provided crucial evidence that the voices were not produced by fraudulent transmissions. However, critics have suggested that even without these two valves it was still technically possible for the radio to produce sound in other wavebands.

Therefore, with the consent of Marcello Bacci, it was decided that in the present experiment all five valves would be removed during the reception of the anomalous voices. Accordingly, approximately one hour after the commencement of the voices and while they were still continuing, Radio Technician Franco Santi leant over the work bench and removed four of the valves, followed after a short pause due to difficulties in handling the hot glass, by the removal of the fifth and last valve. All five valves, ECC85, ECH81 (the two valves removed in the experiment of 2002), EF89 (the intermediate frequency amplifier), EABC80 (the AM/FM detector and low frequency amplifier), and EL84 (the final power amplifier) were then visible outside the radio, and were laid by Franco Santi in full view on the workbench. Despite the absence of the valves, the voices continued with the same volume and clarity as before.

When the voices paused Marcello Bacci, without previous warning and obviously yielding to an impulse, switched off the radio at the set and the light illuminating the glass panel at the front of the set disappeared. After 11 seconds of silence (the timings reported have been taken from the tape recorded during the experiment) the observers could hear modulated whistles (sounds similar to those of whip lashes) and the usual acoustic signal that precedes Bacci's reception of paranormal voices which is similar to a vortex of air. The voice of the invisible communicator, interspersed with whistles, recommenced 21 seconds after Bacci had turned the radio off and continued for 23 seconds (as timed from the audio tape) with the same acoustic quality previously heard, perhaps a little slower but as clear as before. When the speech ended the whistles remained for another 6 seconds while the vortex which was heard at the end of the vocal utterance became weaker and finally disappeared after 12 seconds. However, the contact did not seem to be terminated since another 53 seconds later the vortex could again be heard as well as a very weak male voice which seemed to arise from it and comment the sentence just uttered by Mario Festa "Siete grandi!" (You are great!). The phenomenon lasted for 2 minutes and 20 seconds after the radio was switched off.

During this time Radio Technician Franco Santi inspected the interior of the radio with his pencil torch, the beam of which was briefly visible through the glass panel. This part of the experiment was unplanned, and occasioned particular surprise on the part of the observers. In all three parts of the experiment (radio switched on with valves in place, radio switched on with valves removed, and radio switched off with valves removed) the voices came out unequivocally from the loudspeaker of the radio, and apart from what may have been a slight loss of quality after the radio was switched off, with the same volume and clarity. The radio was then switched back on for a short period, but no further voices were heard during this time, and the experiment was concluded.

Franco Santi then turned the radio through an angle of 90 degrees so that the inside could be closely inspected by all present, with all the room lights now switched on. Dr. Cardoso and Professor Fontana both took photographic evidence of the inside of the radio and of the five valves. Lawyer Amerigo Festa, who also documented the event with his video camera, made a detailed written account of the incidents surrounding and consequent upon Franco Santi removing the valves and Bacci switching off the radio, and this account has been signed as correct by all those present.

Day 20 - Death and the afterlife

Our second to last day will be a lot of talking, for me, and a lot of listening, for you. In fact, although I am going to talk a lot, I will not do the explaining – I have chosen for you a number of quotes, mostly from spirit communicators, describing the process of dying, the nature of the afterlife, and the nature of life in general, which, as we will see, is described to us as much more than the earthly incarnations we know. I have also included some quotes from people who had Near-Death Experiences and Out-of-Body Experiences, to stress how all those who have somehow experienced the *beyond* say exactly the same things.

I will structure my "presentation" around a series of statements – I will provide the statement, a tiny bit of explanation from myself and then a few quotes relevant to that statement chosen amongst the stupendous quantity that is available in the literature. I will not go into great details on the background of who provided the quote and how the quote was obtained - this would be indeed very interesting, but would also keep us here for a long time! Just remember that this "wisdom" has been coming to us from spirit communicators speaking through mediums for the most part of the last two centuries, and that this information has been not only very consistent in terms of substance, but the actual words used to convey it have often been the same, regardless of the location or time, or of the language, culture and religion of either the communicator or of the medium – exactly as it happens for the descriptions provided by the NDErs.

Do you have any questions? Can I go ahead with the first statement?

No, I don't have any questions. I'm just extra-keen to hear about this.

Very good, then. Let's begin from the very basics:

Physical death is not the end of existence.

I believe that most of us think of death as a black curtain that falls and puts an end to everything – our being alive, our being conscious, our having feelings and memories. Basically like falling into a dreamless sleep, or slipping into the drugs-induced coma of anaesthesia before surgery. Only, having died, we won't wake up – that's the end of it, just blackness and nothingness. Well, that is definitely *not* what spirit communicators consistently tell us.

For instance, renowned psychologist Karl Novotny, who had died in Germany in 1965, came through his long time friend Grete Schroeder, who had suddenly and unexpectedly shown automatic writing capabilities, with lessons of psychology and psychiatry, subjects totally unknown to the medium, an accountant by profession. Asked by Schroeder to describe the process of dying, Novotny said:

"It was a spring day, and I was in my country residence, where I rarely go. My health was poor, but I didn't feel the need to stay in bed - on the contrary, I decided to go on a walk with some friends. It was a beautiful evening. Suddenly, I felt very tired and I thought I could not go on. I made an effort to continue, and, all of a sudden, I felt healthy and rested. I quickened my pace, and took in the evening fresh air: I hadn't felt that good in a long time. What happened? Suddenly, I could feel neither tiredness nor the usual laboured breath. I went back towards the friends, who had stopped, and what did I see? I saw myself lying on the ground! My friends were agitated and desperate; one ran to find a doctor. I got near my 'other self' lying on the ground and I looked for the heartbeat: there was no doubt – I was dead! But I felt more alive than ever! I tried to talk to my friends, but they didn't even look at me or bother answering.
So I got angry and went away, but an instant later I was back. It wasn't a pretty sight: all my friends, in tears, who were not taking any notice of me; and that dead body, identical to me, although I felt very good. My dog was yapping in agitation and could not decide whether to come to me or to the other one lying on the ground…

When all formalities were dealt with and my body was put in a coffin I understood I was really dead. I couldn't believe it! I went to see my colleagues at the University, but they could not see me either and didn't answer to my calls. What should I do? I went up the hill where Grete lives. I saw her, alone and sad, but she couldn't see me either. I had to surrender to the truth. The very moment I realized I had left the material world, I saw my mother coming to me with an overjoyed expression on her face and telling me I was in the afterlife."

Nearly one hundred years earlier, the spirit of one Jim Nolan – died during a typhoid epidemic during the American secession war, speaking through medium Mrs. Hollis explained the transition process in very similar terms:

"It was like waking up from a sleep, only with a feeling of bewilderment. I didn't feel ill anymore, and that surprised my greatly. I had a feeling something weird had happened, but couldn't understand exactly what. My body was lying on the bed of the field hospital and I could see it. I told myself 'What a weird phenomenon!' I look around and saw three of my comrades who were killed in the trench and whom I had buried myself. And still, they were there, in front of me! I looked at them with astonishment and one of them greeted me saying: 'Hello Jim, welcome to the spirit world'. I was deeply shaken and said 'My God, what are you saying? I'm not dead…!' 'No', said the other, 'you are more alive than before. But you are in the spirit world. All you have to do to convince yourself is look at your body'."

These two quotes describe a pattern common to any other description of the process of death I have read, and – if you remember – are practically identical to what the NDErs say about their experience: separation of consciousness from the body, awareness of all that goes on in the surrounding environment, impossibility to interact with the physical world and, very often, encounter with deceased loved ones, friends or other spiritual guides. I could bring to you literally dozens of similar quotes, but believe me – the substance is exactly the same: death, as far as we are told, is not a curtain followed by black nothingness.

Ok, point well taken. Now.

Now, time to look at the second statement, which introduces an ethic component in the process. For practicality's sake, we will refer here to disincarnate spirits as "souls".

Following an earthly incarnation, souls undergo some form of judgment.

Initially, this phase is consistently described by NDErs as a life review:

> "The life review was absolutely, positively, everything for the first 33 years of my life... from the first breath of life right through the accident."

> "It proceeded to show me every single event in my life, in a kind of instant three-dimensional panoramic review... The brightness showed me every second of all those years, in exquisite detail, in what seemed only an instant of time."

> "My whole life was there, every instant of it... Everyone and everything I had ever seen and everything that had ever happened was there. "

> "Then I was seeing my whole life from beginning to end, even all those little things you forget along the way."

> "I had a total, complete, clear knowledge of everything that had ever happened in my life – even little minute things I had forgotten"

> "My life passed before me... even things I had forgotten all about. Every single emotion, all the happy times, the sad times, the angry times, the love, the reconciliation – everything was there. Nothing was left out".

But the NDErs go into describing a judgment process that they either carry out themselves or go through with the assistance of higher beings.

> "You are shown your life – and you do the judging."

> "I was asked what had I done to benefit or advance the human race. At the same time, all my life was present instantly in front of me and I was shown or made to understand what counted."

> "[the Being of Light's] love encouraged me to go through my life up to that point. I saw, relived, remembered things that has happened in my life; not only what actually took place, but the emotions involved. [...] I could see for myself and with open eyes and without defenses what actions of mine had caused pain."

204

"Mine was not a review but a reliving. For me, it was a total reliving of *every* thought I had ever thought, *every* word I had ever spoken, and *every* deed I had ever done; *plus* the effect of each thought, word and deed on everyone and anyone who had ever come within my environment or sphere of influence, whether I knew them or not."

"[A prisoner found that a scroll began to unroll before his vision and comments:] And the only pictures on it were the pictures of the people I had injured. There would be no end to it. A vast number of those people I knew or had seen. Then there were hundreds I had never seen. These were people who had been indirectly injured by me. The minute history of my long criminal career was thus relived by me, plus all the small injuries I had inflicted unconsciously. Apparently nothing was omitted in this nightmare of injuries, but the most terrifying thing about it was that every pang of suffering I had caused to others was now felt by me as the scroll unwound itself."

So much for NDErs, but what do people who have actually died have to say? I've come across dozens of quotes from spirit communicators using almost the same words to describe the same process. For instance, in Naples, Italy, Professor Giorgio di Simone of the Italian Parapsychology Society collected and analyzed for over thirty years the recordings of the extraordinary direct voice mediumship of a local medium. Incidentally, some of these recordings were studied by the Electro Acoustics Department of Turin University and compared with recordings of the same sentences pronounced by the medium when not in trance. The conclusion of the laboratory was that "the voices are produced by different individuals". Concerning the life review process, the communicating entity said:

"The dead person 'dreams' all his life, is confronted with all the deeds he did and can take stock exactly of the good or evil, of whether his life was useful or useless. He can weigh each individual deed, linking that to the overall evolution of his soul. Contrary to what it is believed on earth, it is not God passing the judgment, God is not the judge! The judge of the soul is the soul itself."

And from further north in Italy, Florence, where striking materializations and direct voice phenomena characterized for three decades the séances of medium Roberto Setti before he prematurely died in 1984, we learn from one of the communicators:

"When the individual has ceased to exist, he abandons the physical body but remains nearby it for some time and is greatly disturbed by the distress of those left behind. He then goes through a life review and is often helped in this first contact with the spiritual world by people who died before him. [...] Souls painfully relive their misdeeds, and, as a consequence, are purified."

In Paris, France, *circa* 1860, entity *George* communicating through the automatic writing of medium Madame Costel said that:

"Then, the memory of the life he [the deceased] has left behind appears with enormous clarity. This is an experience at times devastating, at times exhilarating, at times consoling. All prejudices are dropped, truth appears in all its brightness and one's soul is seen like in a mirror".

Etcetera. Again, almost identical words across ages and cultures, to describe a very similar process.

OK, point taken as well. What happens afterwards?

The souls, or disincarnate personalities if you prefer, move into the lower levels of non-physical life.

"Lower" levels?

Yes, as we will see shortly, life – we are told – is structured in multiple levels, the earthly incarnations we find ourselves in now being the lowest. More about that in a wee while. Now, let's look at my next statement:

Life in the "lower" levels of the afterlife is experienced differently by different souls. In general, however, it appears similar to life on earth.

Again, let me start with a few of quotes from NDErs.

"To my astonishment, I saw my mum and dad standing only a few steps from me. They were smiling at me (note that I had never really known my mum as she died when I was very young) and they were not talking, but I understood they were telling me not to be afraid. Behind them there was a vast plain, immersed in light, a light of peace, which you understand is eternal, in which living is sweet, a light no human words could even begin to describe."

"I could see a marvellous landscape, a sort of park with extraordinarily bright colours, and in particular an emerald-green lawn with the grass cut short. It was Spring and the lawn was full of small multicoloured flowers I had never seen before. The area was bathed in very bright sunlight, and the colours were of an indescribable splendour. The slope was bordered with trees of a darker green."

"My spirit was wandering in a landscape which might have been painted by Walt Disney. Very green fields, of a tender emerald colour, big leafy trees, enormous, colourful flowers."

"Meanwhile, I was immersed in music that seemed to come out of a sound system in four, five, six dimensions. The sun was pulsating, and I knew that the sun was the divine principle, the alpha and the omega, the source of all energies and all manifestations. What I was seeing was not the sun, but a wonderful apparition similar to the sun - warm, bright. My soul was vibrating in harmony with the vibrations of that sun, and I felt more and more happy and at ease."

And now, let's see what the dead have to tell us. We begin with William Stead, a British journalist who was among the victims of the sinking of the Titanic in 1912. Within minutes from the tragedy, Stead's daughter received a message from her father through automatic writing, in which he announced he was dead and he indicated the exact time at which the transatlantic ship had collided with the iceberg. This, to the young lady's complete shock, happened *before* any information was communicated by radio and newspapers in the UK. In later communications, Stead, who was keen not to talk about his death but rather to describe his experience of the afterlife, said:

"The arrival was marvellous. It was like coming out of a foggy and dark English landscape to find ourselves all of a sudden under the blue Indian sky. Everything was beauty and splendour. We knew that we were approaching the place where these souls, suddenly taken away from earthly life, would find their first home. Something that really surprised me was the colour of the surrounding landscape. It was pale blue, with different shades. I don't mean that everything – trees, houses, people – was blue, but the overall impression was of that colour. Light itself contained an intense blue radiation."

And in the early 1960's, in France, a deceased young man so describes his experience to his mother through the words of a medium:

> "Think of everything we consider magic or enchanting in nature on earth, like water, stars, shells, fireflies and the singing of birds – that is only a pale reflection of our kingdom. Do you remember how I showed an early taste for beauty? It was just an intuition of what was to come. Here everything is shrouded in stars, covered in flowers, scents abound; imagine extraordinary vegetation."

During the first two decades of the 20th century, English medium Ernest H. Peckham received several messages from a spirit, reverend A. H. Stockwell, who had died 40 years earlier. Stockwell provided several details about his life, which Peckham and his group researched and found correct, and said that his mission in the afterlife consisted precisely in communicating to the living information about the afterlife. I would like to use a couple of quotes from him, and the second one will introduce the issue of activities in the afterlife.

Activities?

Hold on a sec, let's hear about the environment.

> "Hearing is such a poor vehicle to channel impressions when compared to seeing. How can one describe the beauty of a sunrise on the Swiss Alps, with its shimmering glory of multiple golden shades, using the chords of a musical instrument? And, how could I accurately and adequately describe to you the glory of spiritual existence using the raw language of the living? The landscape that opened up in front of me was of an incomparable beauty and seemed to expand infinitely in all directions. Above it, a blue sky of a mesmerizing beauty. But the most extraordinary feature of this landscape was that distant objects did not at all appear smaller in size as would be the case on earth. Perspective was literally transformed. And that's not all; as I realized that I could visually perceive objects from all sides at one time and not just from the one visible side as happens in the world of the living. This enhanced, expanded vision produces wondrous effects. When you look at the outer surface of whatever object, you can actually see inside it, around it and through it, because spiritual vision allows you to penetrate the object of observation in its entirety."

And, forgive me, let's leave Rev. Stockwell for a second, because this quote about the enhanced vision has brought to my mind many several similar ones from people describing Out of Body Experiences in the 1970's and 1908's, such as this one:

> "Few objects are visible, but I feel intense energy radiating around me. As I look around, I realize that I don't need to turn my head; I seem to see wherever I direct my thoughts, and I can see in every direction simultaneously; I'm a 360-degree viewpoint without form or substance."

Quite extraordinary, really. I am quite struck, as you said, by the incredible similarities not only of these perceptions, but also of the very words used to describe them.

Yes, you are correct, but to a point. If you go past the general descriptions of fantastic landscapes, shimmering colours, and – especially – of light and warmth associated with an unequivocal feeling of cosmic love, you do indeed find quite some differences among the accounts of life in the lower levels of the afterlife. This is particularly evident when spirit communicators talk about, as I hinted above, the activities they engage in. Let's hear on this very point from Rev. Stockwell.

> "Let me say that there are no two disincarnate personalities who live the same experience. [...] I, for instance, started feeling a need for company; as that feeling grew inside me, I saw the environment around me transforming, expanding, and becoming more beautiful than ever. Then, I started seeing spiritual beings coming towards me from all sides in jubilation. I was to learn afterwards that that miracle was due to my desire for a 'psychic rapport' between me and the other beings on the same spiritual plane."

What do you mean? An environment that's reactive to one's thoughts and desires?

YES! Once more, you've got the essence right away! This is a very consistent trait in the description of the lower spiritual levels, and resonates perfectly with what NDErs and OBErs tell us – at this stage, *we create reality for ourselves*. This is a long, complicated and incredibly fascinating subject, which I have started exploring recently and am just beginning to understand. In fact, it is not only in the afterlife that we seem to interact with and modify the environment we live in. At some stage, you may want to read the phenomenally difficult but equally interesting book by quantum physicist Amit Goswami, *The Self-Aware Universe – How Consciousness Creates the Material World.*

Ouch!

Yes, you're very right – I got carried away. Let's see how other spirit communicators have expressed the same concepts.

> "Ours is a world of thought and everything in it is a creation of thought. Around us creations of our thoughts take form to mingle and harmonize with the creations of other souls' thoughts. Naturally, it is difficult for anybody living on earth to understand this, and still these are simple processes, natural and amazingly effective."

> "So, where does the soul find itself? It is immersed in that particular state of existence that its mental, moral, spiritual condition make possible for it. The environment which welcomes it is determined by the degree of spirituality in which the soul finds itself. Through death, it reaches that spiritual sojourn that it has prepared for itself, and it can't go anywhere else. [...] The future residence is already contained in the soul itself and its spiritual companions are the beings similar to it."

This is incredibly fascinating, but I feel tired, confused. I am sure I am not taking in even a small fraction of all this.

Yes, I know perfectly how you feel now. You have been exposed to so much, such frankly outlandish information, you've had to stretch your faculties of understanding, accepting, taking in... What I'm telling you today takes it all to yet another level – no wonder you feel frazzled. Nevertheless, I think it's important that we talk about such things as we come near the end of our conversations. These subjects, which, as usual, I am just briefly touching upon, deserve in fact a lot of attention and meditation. Whether one believes in the survival of human personality past physical death or not, I think it's immensely interesting and enriching to consider the considerably consistent testimony which comes from such diverse sources, if anything from a purely cultural point of view. Bear with me, then, as we approach the last three statements.

Yes, please, go ahead.

Right then:

There are many levels of the afterlife.

Here again, testimony coming from OBEers, NDErs and spirit communicators is extraordinarily consistent. Many associate different levels of existence to different levels of "vibration", with the earthly plane associated with a "denser", "lower frequency vibration" and the higher levels linked to progressively less "physical", more refined and "higher frequency vibration" realities. Interestingly, we are consistently told that such different levels of reality in fact coexist in the same physical space, much like different radio stations can be found on the same radio frequency band without interacting with one another. Progressing towards higher levels of reality, however, it becomes increasingly clear that time and space are in fact only human illusions.

Although the substance is largely the same, the ways to describe the layered structure of existence differ somewhat from one quote to the next. I just want to give you one comprehensive description, provided by a spirit communicator through direct voice at one of the séances of Roberto Setti in Florence, which I found particularly beautiful.

"The environment in which the individual evolves is composed of the physical plane, the astral plane, the mental plane, the akashic plane and the spiritual planes.

All planes of existence are around you: the world of spirits is within matter itself. But man, when incarnated, cannot perceive more than what his restricted physical senses allow. For every field of existence, the individual has different vehicles or bodies; the astral body is concerned with emotional life, sensations, desires; the mental body gives man all the faculties which are typical of the mind, intellect and thoughts; the akashic body or consciousness receives and transcribes the reality that man discovers and acquires through existence, transforming it in the very nature of the individual.

When the individual has ceased to exist, he abandons the physical body but remains nearby it for some time and is greatly disturbed by the distress of those left behind. He then goes through a life review and is often helped in this first contact with the spiritual world by people who died before him.

The astral world is very similar to the physical world: a very vast and wonderful world inhabited by a great multitude of individuals.

211

The length of time souls spend at this level depends on the degree of spiritual evolution they have reached: evolved souls remain for just a short while, whilst less evolved souls create a virtual world for themselves which enables them to tend to unfulfilled desires; and this until, tired and satisfied, a soul finds itself on the threshold of the next plane, the mental plane, the existence of which it hadn't even imagined until then.

In the mental plane, every creature is immersed in continuous meditation and contemplates experiences of the last incarnation: scientists keep on studying those problems they were not able to solve, so that in the next incarnation they will carry the solutions within themselves. Once all the material accumulated during the last incarnation has been worked through, the individual leaves the mental plane and the faculties he has acquired there are fed into the akashic plane that is the individual's consciousness.

The akashic body retains the imprint of all the experiences lived during the various incarnations and gradually takes shape as the individual evolves. If the individual is not highly evolved, the akashic body is not sufficiently formed and therefore remains on this plane, quietly reviewing all past existences until it is ready for a new incarnation which will further expand his consciousness. If, on the contrary, the akashic body is sufficiently formed, the individual lives a lucid existence centered on the noble sentiments deriving from his acquired consciousness. From this plane of existence he radiates boundless love and limitless compassion towards others.

This is therefore the plane of universal brotherhood and love: the plane where you all will live consciously, understanding that all the difficulties that trouble you now are experiences necessary for your evolution, for your spiritual rebirth. When the individual feels he is at one with the rest of creation, he leaves the akashic plane, getting closer to the very centre of his being, to the divine light, and is ready to reach the spiritual planes and conquer the cosmic, absolute consciousness.

It is very difficult to talk to you, who are living in matter, about spiritual planes; knowing about their existence, however, makes them more easily reachable."

Incidentally, in describing a moment of realization he had during one of his experiences, an OBEr said:

"As I stare at the picture of my life, I realize that the physical events are only a small portion of the whole. I lived in countless different forms, in countless worlds."

This is beautiful. But it is also so completely, utterly beyond my capacity of acceptance right now.

Again, I perfectly understand this. If ever you will want to continue learning about the afterlife, like any other who has gone down this route at some stage you will want to start making sense of what you have learnt – beyond the incredible, the unbelievable which at some stage you may end up accepting. What is all this telling us about the nature of life itself, in this world and in others?
I have embarked myself in this journey, and I can assure you that it is one of immense fascination. A fascination which has culminated, for me, in discovering that the testimony we receive from NDErs, OBErs and spirit communicators on the next, final and absolutely crucial issue *is absolutely identical to what the mystics of all great spiritual traditions have been telling us for the last thirty centuries.*

Uh?

Oh, yes. Please dig into your very last bits of concentration and mental energy, as we are about to take the very final, the ultimate plunge. Let me introduce the last statement.

All is one.

All is one?

Yes, exactly. To begin explaining, let me start by referring to the few words uttered by the Buddha himself, emerging from the altered state in which he attained enlightenment. In describing the ultimate nature of reality, and his experience of it, the Buddha simply said:

Profound calm, free of complexity.
Uncompounded luminosity.

You have to focus on the first line first, and in particular on the words *free of complexity,* which encapsulate much of the ultimate truth. To give you a little push, I'll suggest a very simple image, one that helped me greatly in my early days, and then we will bring in the quotes from a variety of people.

Think of looking at a stormy sea: gigantic waves, each with its own distinctive shape, each moving in a different and complicated matter. Waves crashing on the rocks, dissolving into clouds of droplets, and apparently ceasing to exist. Quite a fitting description of complexity, I believe.

Now, think for a moment – what are the waves? The waves are the sea. The waves are just temporary, superficial manifestations of an underlying, more fundamental reality – the sea. When they crash and apparently dissolve, they simply go back to being what they always had been – the sea. A few meters below the surface of what appears to us as the worst storm there is profound calm, free of complexity. Stay with this image for a moment, if you can.

So, if I were to express the ultimate truth with my own words, I would say that the mesmerizing variety of objects that populate the world – grains of sand, rocks, mountains, planets, stars and, obviously, people – are in fact just temporary, superficial

Appearances – the waves – and reality – the sea. How many times have you heard these concepts already? The Buddhist say that we live in *Samsara,* the world of illusion: we take the material world that we perceive with our senses as reality, whilst it is not. The Hindu speak of the *veil of Maya,* a screen that hides from us the real nature of the world.

What I am trying to tell you here is that mystics, NDErs, OBErs and spirit communicators tell us that that the world of creation "emerges" from an underlying reality of a superior order (a "creator", generally referred to as God) just as waves emerge from the sea. Incidentally – but this is a subject that we *cannot* get into now – this is also precisely what the modern physics is telling us: reality is not the waves, distinct from one another. Reality *is the sea,* undifferentiated, free of complexity. The creator and the creatures are *one*. One NDEr so describes this wonderful truth:

> "It became clear to me that all the higher selves are connected as one being, all humans are connected as one being, we are actually the same being, different aspect of the same being."

And see what a spirit communicator has to say:

> "He is the One that appears as many, but is not appearance, because He is what He is. He is infinite because He is the One, eternal because He is unchangeable, in reality indivisible because in reality He is the only one to exist. He is complete, because He is the Totality that includes everything."

And another, who proclaims:

> "I am a manifestation of the universal force that moulds and brings everything into life."

Believe me, I could go on for quite a while with quotes like those. Instead, let me conclude with a very short review of what the great spiritual traditions of mankind have to tell us. For instance, when the Verse of the Throne says "Allah! There no god but he" it doesn't say, as it is superficially believed, that there are no other gods, it proclaims that the ultimate reality is one - Allah is *all there is*. Similarly, the Jewish *Zorah* tells us that

> "if one contemplates things in mystical meditation, everything is revealed as one",

and the Christian idealist Dionysius writes

> "It is at once in, around and above the world, super-celestial, super-essential, a sun, a star, fire, water, spirit, dew, cloud, stone, rock, all there is".

Meister Ekhart, the thirteen century Dominican monk, wrote:

> "In this breaking-through I receive that I and God are one. Then I am what I was, and then I neither diminish nor increase, for I am then an immovable cause that moves all things".

From the tenth century Sufi mystic Monsoor al-Halaj comes the pronouncement

> "I am the Truth!"

and from eighth-century India, Hindu mystic Shankara inspires us by saying:

> "I am reality without beginning, without equal. I have no part in the illusion of "I" and "you", of "this" and "that". I am *Brahman*, one without a second, bliss without end, the eternal unchanging truth."

And finally, perhaps the most inspiring of the mystics' quotes, the one I found the most beautiful in literary terms and always makes my eyes water, comes from Moses de Leon, a Jewish Kabbalist and probably the author of the *Zorah*:

> "God, when he has just decided to launch upon his work of creation is called *he*. God in the complete unfolding of his Being, Bliss and Love, in which he becomes capable of being perceived by the reason of the heart, is called *you*. But God, in his supreme manifestation, where the fullness of His Being finds its final expression in the last and all-embracing of his attributes, is called *I*".

Day 21 - Conclusion

Dear reader,

I wonder at this point if you have realized that we have spent 20 days, you and me, locked in a special relationship. I wonder if you realized that it was *you* to whom I asked to be an open minded skeptic, *you* have been asking me questions, challenging the pieces of evidence I have presented to you. You, in my wishes and expectations, may have by this time opened up to considering the "unbelievable truth" medium Gordon Smith talks about – that somehow, in a seemingly completely inexplicable way, human personality survives physical death.

If I managed, as I hope, to somewhat arouse your interest and you want to know more about this fascinating subject, there is a colossal literature out there that just waits to be discovered. And, you may perhaps consider trying to get some first-hand experiences. This is what I will try to do myself in the future, as I have been repeatedly told that there is no substitute for direct experience: you may read and study all your life, but then you are exposed to the "real thing" and all that theoretical knowledge is swept away, dwarfed by one gigantic wave of insight.

There is just one last thing that I would like to talk to you about – something that we have briefly touched upon in the early days. I would like to tell you why I embarked in the year-long work of writing this book. I have done this whilst having a day job, and a night job, a lovely wife I adore spending time with (on top of the extraordinary quality time we spend together as musicians), and a son from a previous marriage who lives in another country, who is a promising young football player and whom I try to see at least once a month, and plenty of good friends, and… That is - I am a lucky, happy man, with a busy life, and I had to make a serious effort of discipline and time planning to complete this work in just over a year (from spring 2007 to early summer 2008).

As I said repeatedly, the real effort has been deciding what to select among the incredible mass of evidence I have read about, picking the particular pieces that I thought were most inspiring. Writing comes naturally to me, not unlike teaching and public speaking in general – these things are my *forte*, and even performing music – much as I like it – doesn't come just as easily. So, the real work has been months of feverish consultation of the several thousand pages I have on my bookshelves, and even more feverish reflection on what to choose and how exactly to present it here. The question remains, however – *why did I do it?*

Because I hoped the information contained in this book could be of help to somebody. My fundamental desire to help – the one which brought me to working in the field of humanitarian assistance in the first place – remains as strong as it was 20 years ago. Today I have a different lifestyle, and I would not be ready any more to live in conflict- or disaster-stricken countries, directly providing emergency aid as I did in my early years. But the desire to be of help is still an essential part of me, and such tract of my character has found, in recent years, a natural house in Buddhism. I am today a humble, beginner-level practitioner of the Tibetan school called *Dzogchen*, inspired by the teachings of one of its great living masters, Sogyal Rinpoche. As you may know, compassion and the desire to help are cobblestones that pave the way to spiritual enlightenment in Mahayana Buddhism (to which *Dzogchen* belongs), and trying to disseminate the information contained in this book in the most accessible and interesting way I could was one of my ways to go down that way. You may now understand why I used a Buddhist formula of dedication at the very beginning of this book.

Good, you may say, that's all very nice, but – aren't you simply trying to "convert" people, lead them to believe things that you think are good for them? Well, if you got that impression at this stage, then my approach failed catastrophically, and I must not really be such a great writer! As I said from the beginning, I had no intention whatsoever to convince anybody of anything. I set out to simply present evidence, exactly as I would do in my university class, faced with an intelligent and inquisitive audience whom I know perfectly capable of drawing autonomous conclusions. I hope you will have the patience to follow me with attention for the next – and last – few pages, as I still have some interesting information to share.

What really prompted me to follow this course were the groundbreaking studies carried out since the early 1970's on the psychological and behavioural transformations that people who had a Near Death Experience are consistently showing. We have already mentioned such changes in the chapter on NDEs, but I would like to quote there the brief but systematic review that Dr. Kenneth Ring makes in his book *Lesson from the Light*.

Appreciation for Life

Most NDErs come back into life with a much-enhanced appreciation for everyday life – for the beauty of an old woman's face, for the joys and majestic power of nature, for everday pleasantries in conversation. They see, and see with greater delight, what to many of us has simply become habituation. Their sense of wonder and gratitude for life itself also tends to increase.

Self-Acceptance

Afterward, NDErs come to have greater feelings of self-worth and self-acceptance. Feelings of personal insecurity, shyness, and exaggerated need to please or defer to others are often replaced by a self-confidence and outgoingness that may astonish those who knew them before their NDE.

Concern for Others

One of the most striking and consistent changes following an NDE is an increased and compassionate concern for other persons. To be of service to others is, as one man put it, "more real than this world." To express love for one's fellow humans is to give out a little of what one received in the Light, and the urge to do so is, in some cases, almost unquenchable.

Reverence for Life

Most NDErs find that their concern for others cannot be limited to human beings, but must unhesitatingly extend to all life. So reverence for animal life, for nature, and heightened sensitivity to the ecological health of the planet as a whole tend to characterize the values of many NDErs afterward.

Antimaterialism

Following an NDE, a life centered on materialistic values and acquisition for its own sake tends to be seen as empty and pointless.

Anticompetitiveness

Many NDErs comment that afterward, they can no longer follow the common, socially approved pathways that require one to compete with others for material rewards or success in life. Being somebody important or impressing others ceases to be important. Caring, rather than achieving is what really matters.

Spirituality

Interestingly, many NDErs will say that following their experience, they did not become more religious, but more spiritual. By this, they seem to mean that the formal aspects of religion – in the sense of organized religion – become less important to them and a more universal and inclusive spirituality that embraces everyone comes to exert a deeper hold on their allegiance.

Quest for Knowledge

Many NDErs are imbued with a tremendous thirst for knowledge, which is often put in service of their own spiritual search. To live in accordance with what they learned in the Light, and, toward that end, to somehow recapture some of the knowledge they believe was implanted in them during their experience, become prime motivations for many NDErs.

Sense of Purpose

That life *is* meaningful and that there is a sacred pourpose to everyone's life become deep-rooted convictions for NDErs. Many come to feel that the task of their post-NDE life is to discover their own spiritual *raison d'etre* and thus fulfil their mission in life.

And, what is for me most important,

Fear of Death

The NDE tends to vanquish one's fear of death, completely and forever. While one retains the normal fears associated with the process of dying, the moment of death itself is regarded positively as a liberating transition into a sublime state that NDErs know they have already encountered briefly.

Life after Death

As a rule, NDErs become convinced that some form of sustained conscious existence awaits them following the death of the body. Quite a few of them become more open to or believers in some form of reincarnation.

Again, please remember that this set of "consistent and mutually reinforcing beliefs and values" has been found by many accurately designed psychological and psychometric studies carried out on randomly selected NDErs from different countries, cultures, languages and religious backgrounds. NDEs therefore appear to be capable of transforming everyday behaviour and the overall view of the cosmos. Furthermore, recent research has identified an entire set of previously unknown effects of the NDE that point even more strongly to the conclusion that this phenomenon can in no way be accounted for by purely psychological mechanisms.

Now – isn't this fantastic? Really, wouldn't *you* like to feel a stronger sense of pourpose, greater self-acceptance, greater desire for knowledge and spiritual advancement? Wouldn't *you* be happy to be less afraid of death, not to be tormented by the idea of a switch being flipped and everything you feel you are dissolving into a pitch-black *nothing*?

Well, the good news is that you actually can, and without the need to temporarily die. As I have already mentioned, another set of scientific studies proves that some of the psychological and behavioural changes we've just described become manifest in people who have read about NDEs and dedicated some time to their study – the greater the study effort, the greater the changes. One of these studies, for instance, followed a group of 74 NDErs for psychological and behavioural changes, together with a control group of 54 people who did not have such experience but were interested in the subject and willing to learn. In examining the patterns of belief and value changes, researchers found that the control group showed many of the same effects as the NDErs *since becoming interested in NDEs*, though, not surprisingly, the magnitude of the effects was somewhat smaller than for the NDErs themselves. Nevertheless, the results showed clearly that members of the control group felt they had become more appreciative of life, more self-accepting, more compassionately concerned for others, more spiritual, less materialistic, and so on. Not only that, but further analysis revealed that the shifts in values and outlook reported by the control group tended to persist and did not fade with the passage of time. In some cases, these persons were describing changes that had already lasted two decades.

This, then, was my aim with this book. If learning about NDEs can have such effects, I told myself, learning that there is evidence from at least another dozen fields of investigation that is completely consistent with the indications emerging from NDE research can have an even stronger effect.
It certainly did on me. All I have learnt during my studies on the afterlife resonates perfectly with values that have been mine since I was a child and with the teachings of the spiritual tradition I have chosen to follow (in fact, the very same teachings of humanity, kindness, "positive humbleness" and, especially, concern for others that are at the core of *all* great spiritual traditions of mankind). And, I am not afraid to die any more.

I don't need to "believe" – in fact, I still think that in a way all what we've been discussing is completely, utterly unbelievable. But the sticks are so many (and so many of them are so strong in themselves) that I feel I have crossed the ditch on a pretty solid bridge. I have encountered so many white flies, so absolutely flies and so absolutely white, that I now ready to accept the fact that mind is not limited to the physical brain, and human personality somehow survives physical death.

As I said earlier, I sincerely hope that you have opened up to considering this possibility, and that you will perhaps continue expanding your knowledge in this field. But, most of all, I hope that, whoever you are and whichever are your circumstances, my work will have made your life a tiny bit better.

Namaste.

A big *thank you*

I would like to express my gratitude and appreciation for William Smutz, whose keen editorial eye has helped immensely in making this a truly publishable book.

I would also especially like to thank all those unnamed readers who have "worked the grapevine" to make this a small publishing success.

Please, do not forget to drop me a note with your comments/impressions/suggestions - that'll be very much appreciated! Please write to piero@openmindsite.com

Ground-breaking approach to transforming the fear of death and healing the pain of bereavement.

A new resource addresses the psychological suffering connected with dying and with grieving a loss by rationally considering the evidence for... an afterlife!

A belief that human consciousness and personality go on existing after the death of the physical body is core to practically every major religion. The possibility of life after life is therefore usually dealt with as a matter of faith.

However, a mass of compelling scientific and empirical evidence, gathered for 150 years by some of the brightest scientific minds on the planet, justifies a belief based on reason, rather than on faith. When studied with the care it deserves and with an open, healthy skepticism, such evidence leaves little doubt that, in a manner in which we do not yet understand, human personality indeed survives bodily death.

Medical research shows that studying this evidence and reflecting on its implications can have a dramatic effect in transforming the fear of death and reducing the pain of bereavement.

This is the ground-breaking approach taken by Piero Calvi-Parisetti, a Scottish/Italian medical doctor, psychotherapist and grief counsellor.

> "There is a grim consensus in the grief counselling community – he says – that traditional interventions like talk therapy are useless at best and harmful at worst. On the contrary, studies tell us that bereaved people who rationally consider the evidence for life after life improve significantly, often dramatically."

Dr. Parisetti has been studying and researching the subject for a number of years. A member of the Society for Psychical Research in the UK and of the International Association for Near-Death Studies, in 2008 he published the book 21 Days into the Afterlife, which was translated in six languages and is considered as a classic introduction to the survival hypothesis.

> "As a medical doctor, I want to be of help. I want the knowledge I have accumulated through my passion for psychical research to benefit those who have lost a loved one, and those who are dying."

A former long-time university lecturer, Dr. Parisetti has put some 2,000 hours of work in producing an 8-hour adult education course called Transforming the Fear, Healing the Pain.

> "The course is of academic level, but is delivered in a manner that makes it easy to follow by anybody. It is divided in 30 video modules, each one lasting between ten minutes and half an hour, including lessons and assignments. In each module, I introduce a particular area of evidence for life after life, explain why it is important and discuss possible alternative explanations. The modules also include brief interviews with the leading researchers and other important video footage. The assignments consist of carefully selected sections from some of the best documentaries produced during the last twenty years."

Patient education, also referred to as bibliotherapy, is an established psychotherapy technique, particularly useful in the management of depression and panic attack disorder.

> "I don't want to convince anybody of anything, let alone that there is life after life. I am not in the business of proselytizing – I am in the business of helping people feel better. Countless letters from the readers of my book tell me that when people learn, reflect, and make their own judgment, the do indeed feel better".

A 10-minute video introduction to the course Transforming the Fear, Healing the Grief, together with the first module, are available at: http://drparisetti.com/counselling/bereaved

Dr. Parisetti can be contacted at: piero@drparisetti.com